D1714826

Community Programs for the Health Impaired Elderly

T & A

Community Programs for the Health Impaired Elderly

Ellen D. Taira
Editor

The Haworth Press
New York • London

Community Programs for the Health Impaired Elderly has also been published as *Physical & Occupational Therapy in Geriatrics*, Volume 6, Number 1 1987.

The Haworth Press, Inc., 12 West 32 Street, New York, NY 10001
EUROSPAN/Haworth, 3 Henrietta Street, London WC2E 8LU England

LIBRARY OF CONGRESS
Library of Congress Cataloging-in-Publication Data

Community programs for the health impaired elderly / Ellen D. Taira, editor.
    p. cm.
    Prev. pub. as: Physical & occupational therapy in geriatrics, v. 6, no. 1 1987.
    Includes bibliographies.
    ISBN 0-86656-760-7
    1. Community health services for the aged. 2. Aged — Rehabilitation. I. Taira, Ellen D.
RA564.8.C629   1988
362.1'9897 — dc19   88-2084
                                                                                 CIP

Community Programs
for the Health Impaired Elderly

CONTENTS

ABOUT THE EDITOR

Ellen Dunleavy Taira, OTR, MPH, is affiliated with New York University Medical Center as Assistant Director of the Occupational Therapy Department at Goldwater Memorial Hospital, a 900 bed chronic-care facility in New York City. She has practiced as an occupational therapist specializing in gerontology for more than 20 years with expertise in many areas of long term care. Ms. Taira is the editor of *Physical & Occupational Therapy in Geriatrics*.

FROM THE EDITOR

Devoting a single issue to community programs for the health impaired elderly has been a slow but interesting process. Slow because therapists have only recently begun to carve a place for themselves in community programs. Traditionally, we have found more opportunities for work and professional development in institutional settings. The need for peer interaction and our long attachment to the medical model makes the less structured environment of the community a place of uncertain desirability.

Medicare and Medicaid legislation passed in the mid-sixties only reinforced this inclination since there was little financial support for noninstitutional alternatives such as home care and outpatient services. With the changing reimbursement climate, the increased number of older persons living in the community and, most recently, the DRG and Prospective Payment initiatives, the role of institutions continues to diminish and the press for community alternatives is becoming more urgent with each new directive from government agencies.

Acute hospitals are rapidly expanding their community outreach programs as the length of hospitalization decreases. Concurrently, traditional agencies serving the socially and economically needy

1

funded by the Administration on Aging are expanding their spectrum of services to include the health impaired person who might otherwise need placement in a protected setting.

The objective of this issue of POTG is to begin to define a role for therapists with this expanding population of older persons. Many concerns remain to be addressed at a later date. We have only briefly touched upon the array of services available for the health impaired older person that might be provided by rehabilitation professionals.

Braun and Wake give us an overview of some possibilities for the very frail person who might otherwise require an institutional setting. These are arrangements unfamiliar to most therapists which will become increasingly common as financial support is available. Hoff's program at the VA is a model project that was designed to meet the needs of a select population of veterans. In this model we are also introduced to a new role for therapists, that of case manager.

Two selections address the management of the diabetic in the community. In Smith's article we have a nice example of a single case study and in Woodson's we have a very useful piece of adaptive equipment that is easily provided in an outpatient setting.

The sexual needs of older adults have received little attention in the rehabilitation literature and only recently in the gerontological literature. Fazio helps demystify some common notions about the elderly's desire for information about their changing sexuality.

Housing is one of the crucial components to successful community living for anyone with a health impairment. Yet too often it is considered after the need for support services has been identified. Even more urgent is the need for planners and policy makers to consider affordable, appropriate living situations for older persons with dependency needs.

Lastly, this issue addresses a timely and personal topic for all of us as human beings and therapists: How to cope with the death of a patient. For anyone working with the elderly this is an ever present reality that can be a deterrent for some when opportunities to serve the chronically ill become available. Martin and Berchulc have approached this difficult topic from a thoughtful and sensitive perspective that should be of value to all of us.

This issue is a first attempt to look at the complex issue of providing rehabilitation services in the community. Hopefully, a sequel will follow. Your comments, criticism, and most of all, your own ideas on the subject are always welcome.

EDT

Community Long Term Care: PT/OT Involvement in Patient Rehabilitation and Maintenance

Kathryn L. Braun, DrPH
Wallis Wake, RPT, MPH

SUMMARY. Community programs are being developed to serve frail elders who would otherwise enter nursing homes. Two such programs in Hawaii utilize PT/OT services in caregiver training and in patient care, but are restricted by Medicare and Medicaid reimbursement rules. Thus, physical and occupational therapists in these settings emphasize education of the patient's caregivers and case managers to maintain and monitor patient function and to call for additional PT/OT intervention when appropriate. Past research found slightly better functional improvement in patients in the two community programs as compared to similar patients in nursing homes. This finding suggests that community caregivers can be taught care plans and render treatment recommended by physical and occupational therapists, at least under conditions of professional case management as provided by these programs.

INTRODUCTION

America's elderly population is growing rapidly, especially the portion in need of long term care services (Manton & Soldo, 1985).

Kathryn L. Braun is with the Division of Research, Education, and Quality Assurance, The Queen's Medical Center, 1301 Punchbowl Street, Honolulu, HI 96813. Wallis Wake is Coordinator, St. Francis Home Care Services, St. Francis Medical Center, 2230 Liliha Street, Honolulu, HI 96817.

Data collection was supported by grants from the Henry J. Kaiser Family Foundation of Menlo Park, CA and from the Hawaii State Department of Human Services.

The expansion of community programs is being encouraged in order to decrease dependence on institutional placement of frail elders and to reduce long term care costs (Macken, 1986). At the same time, changes in Medicare reimbursement regulations have led hospitals to discharge elders "quicker and sicker," admitting them to long term care facilities, home care, and community programs at higher levels of need for nursing and therapeutic services (Grazier, 1986). Thus, physical and occupational therapists may be increasingly called upon to serve frail elders in home and community long term care settings.

Honolulu has several community programs designed to substitute for skilled nursing (SNF) and intermediate (ICF) facility care of selected frail elders, two of which are presented here. They are the Community Care Program of The Queen's Medical Center and the Nursing Home Without Walls Program of Hawaii's Department of Human Services. The development of these "institutional alternatives" was encouraged by Hawaii's Medicaid program primarily because of the high cost of Hawaii nursing homes, among the most expensive in the country (Institute of Medicine, 1986).

This paper describes Hawaii nursing homes and the two alternative programs, outlines the extent of PT/OT involvement in the three settings, and reviews the results of past research on patient function in the three settings.

THE THREE LONG TERM CARE SETTINGS

Hawaii Nursing Homes

Hawaii nursing homes play a key role in the care of frail elders, as do nursing homes in most states. Hawaii's Department of Health certifies three types of beds: skilled, intermediate, and swing (which can accommodate either a skilled or intermediate patient, eliminating the need to transfer a patient as his care needs change). In 1986, Hawaii had 33 nursing homes with 621 skilled beds, 959 intermediate beds, and 1168 swing beds. Data presented by the Institute of Medicine (1986) shows that in 1982 Hawaii's daily ICF reimbursement rate was $58 (compared to $36 nationally) and its daily SNF reimbursement rate was $72 (compared to $43 nationally). This high cost may be due to the low ratio of nursing home beds per licensed nurse, 4.8 in Hawaii compared to 9.8 nationally. In addition, Hawaii has relatively few beds per 1000 people 65 and older, 19.3 compared to a national average of 55.8 (Institute of Medicine, 1986).

PT/OT Involvement

For patients in nursing homes, physical and occupational therapists can be reimbursed by Medicare or Medicaid as long as the condition of skilled care is met. Rehabilitation is considered skilled when the provider can document significant patient progress in a reasonable period of time. Under Medicare guidelines, no definite parameters are given regarding the meaning of "significant patient progress" or "reasonable period of time." However, activities such as repetitive ambulation, range-of-motion, and maintenance exercises which can be administered by nontherapy personnel and do not lead to significant patient progress are not considered skilled care and are not reimbursed by third party payers. Most nursing homes offer arts and crafts programs and encourage daily ambulation schedules to help maintain patient coordination and mobility. These services can be provided by aides and volunteers under the professional supervision of nurses.

The Community Care Program

Established in 1979, the Community Care Program of The Queen's Medical Center in Honolulu provides geriatric foster care. This program recruits, trains, and supervises foster families who "adopt" and care for one or two unrelated elderly people who would otherwise enter nursing homes. It was patterned after similar programs at the Johns Hopkins Hospital in Baltimore and the Massachusetts General Hospital in Boston. The reader is referred elsewhere for case illustrations, a satisfaction study, and program history (Braun et al., 1985; Braun & Rose, 1987b; Vandivort et al., 1984). Program processes are summarized and updated here. (See Photograph 1.)

PHOTOGRAPH 1. Violet Souza with foster caregiver Betty Barroga

Funding

During its early years, the Community Care Program staff salaries were funded by the medical center while money to pay foster families was obtained from local trusts and foundations. In 1981, the Health Care Financing Administration (HCFA) introduced 2176 Home and Community Based Services Waivers authorizing States to use Medicaid funds for noninstitutional services to disabled people eligible for Medicaid-funded nursing home care. The Community Care Program received such a waiver which has allowed Medicaid payment for most foster care services since 1984.

Foster families provide room and board, housekeeping, and personal care for which they receive between $600 and $900 a month. Medicaid pays a portion of this cost for eligible patients. In addition, The Queen's Medical Center receives $380 per month for case management services, the total cost of which is borne by Medicaid for eligible patients. In Fiscal Year 1986, foster care services cost Medicaid an average of $900 per patient month. Patients who are not eligible for Medicaid may pay privately for this care.

Selecting Families

Potential foster families are evaluated carefully through a written application process, personal interviews, references, and a home evaluation. At the very least, foster families must have a bedroom exclusively for the patient; provide 24-hour supervision of the patient; include the patient in the family's daily routine; follow the patient's care plan; and have another source of family income. The majority of foster family caregivers have had experience/training in caregiving either at home or in health care facilities. From the Community Care Program they receive an additional 12 hours of group training in geriatrics and gerontology as well as individualized training in the needs of their specific clients.

Selecting Patients

Potential patients must be certified for nursing home entry and must be age 55 or older. Patients are assessed for their ability to fit into a family care setting and their willingness to try foster family care. Other than this, patients may have extensive disabilities. Placement depends on the availability of a foster family able to meet the patient's physical care and social needs. Currently, 45 patients are participating in this program.

Case Management and Personal Care

The decision to place a patient in a foster home depends on mutual agreement by the patient and his family, his physician, the foster family, and the case management team. The case management team, consisting of a registered nurse and master's prepared social worker, oversees all patient and family selection and matching. They maintain the foster family/patient system through regular home visits and telephone calls to assure that the patient's plan of care is followed, to monitor the patient's condition and needs, to arrange other health, social, and financial services as needed, to communicate with the physician and other involved parties, and to assist the patient and family with adjustment and well-being. Personal care is provided by the foster caregiver and includes assistance with Activities of Daily Living (ADL), mobility, maintenance and strengthening exercises, medications and nursing needs (if the foster caregiver is also a licensed professional), and transportation.

PT/OT Involvement

Included in the foster family group training is instruction by a physical therapist. When ordered by a physician, individualized physical and occupational assessment and treatment can be provided to a patient. As in the nursing home, however, the condition of skilled care must be met for reimbursement of outpatient or in-home services from physical and occupational therapists to foster care patients. In the initial home visit, professionals assess the patient and the home setting, identify problems, recommend actions to correct problems, and establish short and long term goals in consultation with the patient and foster caregiver. During each visit the caregiver receives instruction in the specific therapeutic needs of the patient. Once the patient's condition begins to stabilize and skilled care is no longer needed, it is the responsibility of the foster caregiver to continue the patient's personalized treatment program to prevent further deterioration. Caregiver compliance with the treatment plan and patient status are monitored by the foster program case managers.

Nursing Home Without Walls

Comprehensive home services are provided in the homes of patients certified for nursing home entry by Hawaii's Nursing Home Without Walls Program (NHWW), established in 1983. The program uses case management teams to orchestrate the delivery of several services including: personal care, transportation, adult day health care, skilled nursing, homemaker services, emergency alarm systems, home modifications, home delivered meals, nutritional counseling, and respite. Reports of patient satisfaction and case illustrations appear elsewhere (Braun et al., 1987; Goto & Braun, 1987). Program processes are summarized and updated here. (See Photograph 2.)

Funding

NHWW is administered by the Community Long Term Care Branch of Hawaii's Department of Social Services and Housing under a 2176 Medicaid Waiver. Services are available to Hawaii residents of any age who are certified in need of SNF or ICF care; are eligible for Medicaid reimbursement; and can be safely cared for at home through a case-managed plan of services costing no more than 75% of the average per patient Medicaid cost of institutional care. Private paying patients are not accommodated, nor are live-in family caregivers paid to provide care to their patients. In

PHOTOGRAPH 2. Mrs. Yaiko Kuraya with NHWW aide Lianne Shiroma

Fiscal Year 1986, services cost Hawaii's Medicaid Program an average of $1350 a month.

Selecting Patients

Patients are referred to NHWW from hospitals, home health care agencies, nursing homes, physicians, and families. The admissions case management team assesses each referral for eligibility (level of care and Medicaid), family caregiver support, home safety, patient care needs, and availability of needed services. The great majority of patients live with family caregivers who provide the bulk of the care, especially at night and on weekends. NHWW services complement the care provided by families. About 160 patients are currently participating.

Case Management and Personal Care

Once the services are in place, the case is assigned to another case management team which continues to orchestrate the delivery of relevant services, making changes as needed. All NHWW patients receive case management services which are provided either in an intensive or primary form, depending on the amount of monitoring, assistance, and counseling needed by the patient and his caregiver. All case management teams consist of a registered nurse, a medical social worker, and a social service aide. The teams work with each patient's private physician and with the program's physician consultant.

About 85% of all patients receive personal care, delivered by personal care aides who have received over 200 hours of classroom and field training from NHWW trainers. Personal care services include assistance with ADL and mobility. The personal care aides also provide some homemaker services. These aides are supervised by the case management teams. In addition to case management and personal care, program funds are used by 35% of the NHWW clients for transportation services, by 15% for adult day health care, and by 10% to modify their homes (build wheelchair ramps, widen doorways). Less than 10% use the other available services.

PT/OT Involvement

Physician referral is also a prerequisite for PT/OT services that are skilled and reimbursed by third party payers in this setting. As in foster care, PT/OT involvement includes assessment of the patient in the home setting, the preparation of a care plan, recommendations for home modifications, and instruction of the caregiver and/or NHWW aide. Further treatment is reimbursed as long as it meets the skilled condition. The instruction component is crucial because physical and occupational therapists will not be reimbursed for continued visits once the patient's progress plateaus. Thus, professionals must impart to the family caregiver and the NHWW aide the importance of administering an effective home exercise program, of maintaining the patient's equipment, and of using proper body mechanics when assisting the patient in ADL and mobility. Again, patient progress and caregiver/aide compliance with the care plan are monitored by the NHWW case managers.

PREVIOUS RESEARCH

Research on patients in the three settings, and on caregivers in the two community programs, began in 1982 and has addressed a number of research questions. Findings on patient function studies, of primary interest to physical and occupational therapists, are reviewed here.

A longitudinal study began in 1982 in which data were collected on 352 patients who were at least 55 years old, certified to need nursing home care, and admitted to one of the three settings: 131 patients in nursing homes; 138 in foster homes; and 83 receiving NHWW services at home. The nursing home sample was admitted directly from The Queen's Medical Center between 1982 and 1985. The foster care sample included all admissions between 1979 and 1986; about 95% were admitted from hospitals. The NHWW sample included all admissions between 1985 and 1986; about half were admitted from hospitals.

Patient data collected included: age, type and number of chronic conditions, mental status, and need for assistance in ADL and mobility items. The Katz Index of Activities of Daily Living (ADL) was used to measure their extent of functional disability (Katz et al., 1972). Specifically, patients were rated in bathing, dressing, toileting, continence, feeding, transfer and going outside using a three-point scale, and in ambulation using a six-point scale. For matching and outcome purposes, the item scores were summed into two total scores. The first six items were summed into an ADL score, from six (independent in six items) to 18 (dependent in the six items). The last two items were summed into a mobility score, from two (independent in both items) to nine (dependent in both items). Mental status was collected using the Orientation portion of the Vigor, Intactness, Relationships, and Orientation (VIRO) scale developed by Kastenbaum and Sherwood (1972). Six answers were solicited: patient's age or date of birth; the current day, month, and year; and the name and location of the interview site. The range of possible scores is zero (no correct answers) to 18 (all correct answers).

Comparison of Patient Characteristics

Selected characteristics of patients in the three settings were compared using ANOVA and chi-square techniques. As shown in Table 1, the mean age of patients and the proportion 85 years of age and older differed among the three long term care settings. The NHWW program had the greatest proportion of very old patients (almost half), followed by nursing homes (one-third) and foster care (one-quarter). Mean scores on ADL and mobility also differed significantly among the three settings, with the most disabled elders entering nursing homes, and the least disabled elders in foster care. Mental status was measured in two ways. More nursing homes patients had dementia and, as a group, they had significantly lower orientation scores compared to patients in the community settings. Patients had between three and four chronic conditions; this item did not differ among settings.

Table 2 displays the ADL and mobility item scores of the patients upon their admissions to nursing homes and community long term care settings. Compared to patients in the two community settings, greater proportions of patients in nursing homes were totally depen-

Table 1. Characteristics of Patients in Nursing Home and
Community Long Term Care Settings

	Nursing Homes (N=131)	Foster Care (N=138)	NHWW (Own Home) (N=83)	Significance Probability of Difference	
				ANOVA	χ^2
Age					
Mean age (years)	80	77	81	*	
% 85/older	34%	19%	46%		***
Admission Scores[a]					
Mean ADL	14.4	12.7	13.2	***	
Mean mobility	6.7	6.4	6.5	**	
Mental Status:					
Orientation score[b]	6.4	10.3	9.2	***	
% with dementia	45%	28%	25%		**
Mean diagnoses	3.5	3 .2	3.5		

[a] A lower score indicates better function.
[b] A higher score indicates better function.
* p < .05
** p < .01
*** p < .001

dent in bathing, dressing, toileting, continence, feeding, and walking, and were confined to the house.

A large number of disabled patients, however, were served in the community settings. For example, 65-71% of patients in the three community settings needed assistance in bathing and 66-76% of them needed assistance in dressing. Only 13-17% of the community patients were completely independent in toileting, only 31-37% were rarely or never incontinent, only 39-44% were independent in feeding, only 20-24% were independent in their transfers, and only 27-36% did not need human assistance with ambulation.

Evaluation of Outcomes

Previous work compared three-month outcomes of 49 matched triads of patients in the three settings. Since patients in the three settings were different on several characteristics, matching was

Table 2. Activities of Daily Living and Mobility Skills of Patients in Nursing Homes and Community Long Term Care Settings.

	Nursing Homes (N=131) N (%)	Foster Care (N=138) N (%)	NHWW/PCP (Home Care) (N=83) N (%)	Significance Probability of Difference χ^2
Bathing				
independent	1 (1)	9 (7)	2 (2)	
needs some help	15 (11)	38 (28)	22 (27)	
bathed by others	115 (88)	91 (65)	59 (71)	***
Dressing				
independent	1 (1)	15 (11)	4 (5)	
needs some help	16 (12)	32 (23)	16 (19)	
dressed by others	114 (87)	91 (66)	63 (76)	***
Toileting				
independent	12 (9)	24 (17)	11 (13)	
needs some help	58 (44)	86 (62)	49 (59)	
toileted by others	61 (47)	28 (21)	23 (28)	***
Incontinence				
never or rarely	19 (15)	43 (31)	31 (37)	
at least once a week	39 (30)	46 (33)	20 (24)	
daily	73 (55)	49 (36)	32 (39)	***
Feeding				
independent	43 (33)	61 (44)	32 (39)	
needs some help	52 (40)	62 (45)	33 (40)	
fed by others	36 (27)	15 (11)	18 (21)	*
Transfer				
independent	12 (9)	28 (20)	20 (24)	
needs assistance	112 (85)	110 (80)	51 (62)	
bedbound	7 (6)	0 (0)	12 (14)	***
Ambulation				
independent	10 (7)	19 (14)	6 (7)	
with cane	1 (1)	6 (4)	4 (5)	
with walker	14 (11)	25 (18)	12 (15)	
with human help	53 (40)	61 (44)	29 (34)	
wheelchair	39 (30)	21 (15)	19 (23)	
gerichair or bedbound	14 (11)	7 (5)	13 (16)	*
Going Outside				
>2 days in 2 weeks	15 (12)	17 (12)	18 (22)	
1-2 days in 2 weeks	28 (21)	44 (32)	14 (17)	
less than biweekly	88 (67)	77 (56)	51 (61)	*

*   p < .05
*** p < .001

done to control for the differences before comparing the outcomes. The matched subjects were selected from the 269 patients who had stayed at least three months in their respective settings (101 in nursing homes, 100 in foster homes, and 68 with the NHWW program). These patients were similar in age and were matched on their admission scores in ADL, mobility, and mental status. After three months, patients in the two community settings showed significant improvement over time in most ADL and mobility items while patients in nursing homes showed significant improvement in only two items. Comparing their three-month scores, however, the three-way differences were significant in only two items — dressing and house confinement — indicating better function for the community patients. Types and incidence of morbidity were similar; however, patients in the community settings expressed greater well-being and entailed lower costs for their routine care (Braun & Rose, 1987a).

DISCUSSION

PT/OT Involvement with Community Patients

A number of commonalities surfaced for physical and occupational therapists working with these two community programs. For example, the two programs have similar restrictions on the use of physical and occupational therapists. Their patients had similarly high levels of dependence in ADL and mobility skills. Finally, the therapists provided the same kinds of services in the two settings, focusing on assessment, home modification, and training.

The first area was the assessment of the patient in his own home environment. For patients at home, the problem areas best identified and addressed by physical therapists included: (1) bed mobility (including supine to sitting); (2) specific dynamics of transfers (sitting to standing, transfers involving the toilet or bedside commode, transfers into the shower or tub, and transfers to wheelchair or parlor chair); (3) wheelchair or ambulatory mobility in limited space; and (4) ambulation over uneven surfaces, both indoors and outside. Problem areas best identified and addressed by occupational therapists included patient deficiencies in dressing, grooming, bathing, and eating within his own home setting.

A second area of focus for physical and occupational therapists involved with the community patients was home modifications. Both therapists have special skills to address home modifications and home safety issues for individual patients and their caregivers.

There are a variety of ways to adapt a home and devise equipment. For example, the combination of a kitchen chair with "ski" feet and a rubber mat may work as effectively as a manufactured shower bench to increase safety and facilitate bathing at reduced patient expense. Journal articles sharing successful home adaption techniques would benefit practitioners working with community programs.

Physical and occupational therapists providing home care must also be teachers. Therapists must often help a family caregiver understand the patient's illness and his potential for regaining function. Once realistic goals are agreed upon, the therapist must work with the patient and caregivers to develop a care plan which will be followed. The next goal is to make the caregiver feel competent in handling the patient and any new equipment. Return demonstrations are very effective here. Finally, the caregiver needs to know what to expect in terms of patient progress. They should know to report any unexpected patient changes in function to the attending physician and to the case manager from the community program. Further intervention by physical and occupational therapists may be appropriate and may help restore the patient to former functional levels.

To facilitate appropriate referrals of community patients, physical and occupational therapists should continue educational efforts aimed at other providers involved in elder care. Most nurses and social workers do not have special training in rehabilitation and maintenance of function. Yet, in most community programs they are given the responsibility to monitor patient progress in these areas. They need to know the questions to ask caregivers so that they can determine when PT/OT services are appropriate. They also need to have avenues through which to get advice about when to pursue a particular PT/OT referral.

Effectiveness of the Community Programs

In terms of the maintenance of function, past research findings suggest that the caregivers in the community settings were able to adhere to treatment regimes recommended by physical and occupational therapists. This may reflect a history of successful PT/OT involvement with the programs and the effectiveness of the case management components of the two community programs. Specifically, case managers participate in the PT/OT segment of caregiver training. Case managers visit patients and their caregivers regularly. Patients are reassessed regularly and as needed. Caregivers are encouraged to report patient illness, accident, and change in patient function in a timely manner. Since case management is reimbursed on a monthly basis, the number of monthly visits and telephone contacts are not restricted. Thus, the knowledge level of the case managers and the frequency of their home visits may have encouraged patients and caregivers in the continuation of scheduled exercises, the proper use of equipment, and the prompt reporting of changes impacting patient independence.

CONCLUSION

This paper described two community long term care programs in Hawaii which serve disabled elders. PT and OT services to patients in these two settings were restricted by financing mechanisms but usually included: assessment of the patient, identification of problems, development of short and long term goals, recommendations for home modifications, and training of the caregiver in the patient plan of care and in transfer techniques. In addition, physical and occupational therapists were involved in the pre-placement training of caregivers and case managers to sensitize them to the common problems which can discourage progress in functional independence among patients in home settings.

Past research showed that the majority of patients served by these two community programs were disabled in ADL and mobility, although in smaller proportions than patients in nursing homes. To compare patient outcomes, pre-admission differences were controlled using a "matched triad" design. After three months in placement, patients in the community programs showed greater improvement in more ADL and mobility items than did their matched counterparts in nursing homes. This finding suggests that the community programs can maintain patient function. Regular attention by case managers, a built-in feature of both community programs, may encourage patient and caregiver compliance with PT/OT care plans.

Physical and occupational professionals should be alert to community and home-based programs developing in their locales. Although rules vary among states, physical and occupational therapists are usually reimbursed to serve long term care patients in noninstitutional settings. Working together with program case management teams may enhance PT/OT impact on patients in community long term care programs.

REFERENCES

Braun, K.L., Goto, L.S., & Lenzer, A.M. (1987). Patient age and satisfaction with home care. *Home Health Care Services Quarterly*, in press.

Braun, K.L., & Rose, C.L. (1987b). Family perceptions of geriatric foster family and nursing home care. *Family Relations, 36*, 321-327.

Braun, K.L., & Rose, C.L. (1987a). Geriatric patient outcomes and costs in three settings: Nursing home, foster family, and own home. *Journal of the American Geriatrics Society, 35*, 387-397.

Braun, K.L., Vandivort, R.E., & Kurren, G.M. (1985). Foster care is a workable option in Hawaii. *Perspectives on Aging, 9(1)*, 18-20, 25.

Goto, L.S., & Braun, K.L. (1987). Nursing Home Without Walls: An alternative to nursing home placement. *Journal of Gerontological Nursing, 13(1)*, 7-9.

Grazier, K.L. (1986). The impact of reimbursement policy on home health care. *Pride Institute Journal of Long Term Home Health Care, 5(1)*, 12-16.

Institute of Medicine. (1986). *Improving the quality of care in nursing homes*. Washington, DC: National Academy Press.

Kastenbaum, R., & Sherwood, S. (1972). VIRO: A scale for assessing interview behavior of elderly people. In D.P. Kent, R. Kastenbaum, & S. Sherwood (Eds.), *Research, planning and action for the elderly*. New York: Behavioral Publications.

Katz, S., Ford, A.B., Downs, T.D., Adams, M., & Insby, D. (1972). *Effects of continued care: A study of chronic illness in the home*. DHEW Publication 73-3010, Washington, DC: Government Printing Office.

Macken, C.L. (1986). A profile of functionally impaired elderly persons living in the community. *Health Care Financing Review, 7(4)*, 33-49.

Manton, K.G., & Soldo, B.J. (1985). Dynamics of health changes in the oldest old: New perspectives and evidence. *Milbank Memorial Fund Quarterly/ Health and Society, 63(2)*, 206-85.

Vandivort, R.E., Kurren, G.M., & Braun, K.L. (1984). Foster family care for frail elderly: A cost-effective quality care alternative. *Journal of Gerontological Social Work, 7*, 101-104.

The Occupational Therapist
as Case Manager
in an Adult Day Health Care Setting

Sherry Hoff, OTR, RN

SUMMARY. Adult Day Health Care (ADHC) is a new Veterans Administration Research Program designed to offer elderly veterans day hospital and rehabilitative care to prevent nursing home placement. ADHC is the liaison between the hospital and the community with care provided by an interdisciplinary team using the case manager approach. This article reviews the program and the role of the ADHC occupational therapist. It illustrates the expanded responsibilities that are encompassed in the position of occupational therapist as case manager.

The Veterans Administration (VA) central office estimates that by the year 2000 there will be nine million veterans over the age of 65, and of that number 25% will receive their primary health care from the VA (Veterans Administration, 1984). Currently, the VA provides health care for 825,000 veterans, of which 20,000 are residing in VA nursing homes or VA contract nursing homes (Veterans Administration, 1984). Adult Day Health Care (ADHC) is a new, federally funded program located originally in four United States sites. It has been developed to provide health care in a cost-effective manner for the frail elderly in a day hospital rather than a

Sherry Hoff is affiliated with Portland VA Medical Center, Portland, OR. She is also American Occupational Therapy Association Gerontology Liaison for the State of Oregon. Correspondence may be addressed to: Sherry Hoff, Rehabilitation Medicine (117-V), Portland VA Medical Center, PO Box 1035, Portland, OR 97207.

more restrictive institutional setting and eliminates the need for other community services.

The ADHC program of the Portland Veterans Administration Medical Center opened in June of 1985. ADHC is an innovative approach to care of the frail elderly who have complex health care needs which would otherwise necessitate their placement in nursing home settings. It is also a therapeutically oriented day program which provides health maintenance and rehabilitative services to elderly individuals in a congregate setting of approximately five hours per day, two or three days per week. The veterans attend the program for six months and are then discharged to home and other community resources. Attendance is Monday/Wednesday or Tuesday/Thursday. Distinction is made by cognitive status; the memory impaired attend Tuesdays and Thursdays. All veterans needing three-day-per-week programming attend on Fridays. The average age of the veteran at this ADHC is 80. Of 20-25 veterans in daily attendance, one or two typically are women. Ninety-five veterans have been admitted to this program, currently 60 attend per week. All require assistance in some form of activities of daily living (ADL) and half are dependent in toileting and ambulation.

STAFFING AND CRITERIA FOR ADMISSION

The program is staffed by a core of 8.5 full-time employees. A coordinator with a MS in Nursing, a nurse practitioner, social worker, two LPN's and a secretary form the full-time staff. Occupational therapy, corrective therapy, psychology, and recreation therapy are half-time positions.[1] A dietitian is .3 FTE and the geriatrician .2 FTE.[2] The geriatrician acts as Medical Director. Thus, the program offers physical examinations as required, monitoring of medication and health status by the nurse practitioner and physician, and medication administration including dispensing medications into home cassettes. Also provided are catheter care, dressing changes, and health monitoring by the nursing staff.

Presently, to be eligible the veteran must have a service-connected illness for the condition requiring treatment, 50% service-connected or more for any condition, or be a nonservice-connected veteran in a VA hospital or nursing home care unit.[3]

Admission criteria (Veterans Administration, 1987) is as follows:

1. Not in acute medical distress.
2. Veteran would, without ADHC services, most probably be in a nursing home. This condition is met if the patient meets one of the following criteria:
   a. Nursing Home Residency: Currently is a nursing home resident.
   b. Toileting: Receives personal assistance in cleansing self and redressing after toileting.
   c. Ambulation: Does not walk more than 20 feet without personal assistance or does not wheel more than 50 yards without assistance.
   d. Cognition: Has significant cognitive impairment as indicated by a score of 21 or less (out of 30) on the Mini Mental State Exam.
3. Most of the veteran's health care needs can be met in the ADHC without the need for VA outpatient services.
4. Veteran has a supportive living arrangement sufficient to meet his/her health care needs when not at ADHC.
5. Suitable transportation can be arranged between the veteran's home and the ADHC.
6. Veteran lives no further than one hour's travel time from the ADHC.
7. Able to benefit from interdisciplinary care of his/her chronic health problem.
8. Screened by ADHC staff.

Research into the medical efficacy, patient/caregiver satisfaction and cost-effectiveness of this program is due to begin in Spring 1987. After that time, eligibility and admission criteria may be amended according to the study results.

CASE MANAGEMENT AND PROGRAMMING

Prior to opening, the ADHC staff agreed that the most effective approach to the care of the elderly would be achieved through the team concept. It was agreed that duties generic to all attendees would be administered by all staff. These include greeting upon arrival with refreshment and socialization, assisting with ambulation and toileting, distribution and set up of lunch trays and eating assistance as required, preparation for rest, and assistance in departure including donning coats and safe disposition to waiting vehicles. In these jobs all staff are equal. Staff members with skills in the above areas are responsible for training and monitoring other staff including affiliating students in nursing, occupational therapy, social work, psychology, and art therapy. The corrective therapist teaches safe ambulation and transfer techniques. The occupational therapist teaches set-up for optimum patient independence in grooming and eating. For example, tips on chair positioning of the cognitively disabled so they can sit closer to their plate. The occupational therapist also offers guidelines for successful geriatric task groups following the training manual of Ross and Burdick (Ross & Burdick, 1981).

After a veteran is accepted into the program, a member of the staff is assigned as their case manager. The case manager is the personal advocate for the veteran; this is similar to primary nurse management of hospitalized persons. The case manager does an initial patient screen, leads the interdisciplinary team in preparing and regularly updating a comprehensive treatment plan, monitors intervention by other team members, and is the family/caregiver liaison.

As case manager it is frequently necessary to communicate regularly with the veteran and also his closest family and/or caregiver. Case management means coordinating all information regarding medications, health, financial status, adequacy of home care, caregiver fatigue, ADL, and environment and relaying that information to the appropriate staff person for intervention. Concerns regarding community resources are handled by the case manager in consultation with the social worker.

Veterans attend a one-hour group session each morning and afternoon. One of these groups emphasizes range of motion type physical activity. The other is cognitive or sensory depending on the requirements of the members. There may be as many as three concurrent groups. Examples of a typical Wednesday might be an exercise group, nutrition group and an occupational therapy stroke group in the morning with a cognitive retraining group and a balloon volleyball game in the afternoon. Interspersed are individual interventions such as nursing treatments, baths, corrective therapy workouts, counseling sessions, occupational therapy evaluations, and recreational therapy leisure assessments. Use of space and equipment is designed to encourage social interaction and support between veterans. This promotes a therapeutic milieu that emphasizes each veteran's strengths.

OCCUPATIONAL THERAPY

The occupational therapist works four hours a day Monday through Friday. Occupational therapy is provided on many levels. All veterans are screened initially by the occupational therapist as part of the acceptance criteria for level of ADL and IADL, (Instrumental Activities of Daily Living) using the Barthel Index (Mahoney & Barthel, 1965; Hasselkus, 1982). Activities of daily living are defined as those tasks involved in personal care such as eating, grooming, dressing, bathing, and toileting. Instrumental activities of daily living are then all other tasks "instrumental" to independent living such as food preparation, shopping, money management, and transportation. In addition to the ADL assessment, as a primary group organizer the occupational therapist evaluates the potential client for group compatibility.

The occupational therapist and the corrective therapist coordinate therapy directed at improving all areas of ADL including dressing training and range of motion programs for hemiplegic patients and bathroom transfers and mobility. When a veteran is able to dress, eat, groom, and ambulate without help the staff is informed and then encouraged to allow the veteran independence in this activity. The occupational therapist offers suggestions for improved self-help in all areas ranging from joint protection of arthritic hands to organizing sensory integrative tasks that improve attention span and eye-hand coordination of cognitively disabled veterans. In addition, a regular column is printed in the monthly newsletter called "Easy Living" containing suggestions for all older persons. The psychologist along with the social worker facilitate patient and family education and counseling both in a monthly group and individual sessions.

Home evaluations are done by all staff. When there are questions concerning environmental barriers, the occupational and corrective therapists either consult or carry out the evaluation. Such as in the case of the blind veteran living with his elderly spouse who benefits from suggestions on positioning furniture to optimize his safety and ambulatory independence. Or, the caregiver who needs to learn and practice unique transfers to make the bathroom of an older home accessible. Equipment is issued when needed. The older veteran does not seem to readily accept adaptive aids but tub-seats, grab bars, and flexi-shower hoses are always welcome.

The occupational therapist plans and leads one group each day. Group content always includes sensory integration and some form of cognitive stimulation. This may be chair exercises, cooking, art, or ADL practice. The most successful groups have been nostalgic activities such as churning butter, pulling taffy, and donning vintage hats (see Photograph 1). The men are very receptive to wood projects. They have sanded and assembled many pre-sawed projects including planters and bird feeders. Some of these have been "Community Projects" worked on by all veterans and benefiting the community. These include an oak music stand on wheels made for the chaplain who was constantly dropping his music while leading prayer and singing groups. Also lovingly crafted were 40 small wooden toys which were presented to disadvantaged children at Christmas. The veterans contribute favorite poems, jokes, and original verse to their monthly newsletter which is edited and published by an ADHC staff member.

The occupational therapist at this ADHC is the case manager for five veterans. Bearing in mind that this is a half-time position, what is new to occupational therapy and also most time-consuming is the increased number of phone calls. Calls are made to and from the

PHOTOGRAPH 1. Hat Day

veterans, their caregivers, and other community resources. Communication is also necessary within the VA system to appropriate disciplines and offices. ADHC initiates outgoing information concerning scheduling and programming but the greatest bulk of communication seems to come from the veteran's home especially as the staff and case manager become trusted. An added dimension is that often the veteran's caregiver is equally as disabled as the veteran, either cognitively or physically. Thus the case manager sometimes provides intervention to the caregiver, to better assist the veteran.

The most common issues revolve around medications, falls, bowels, bathing, skin conditions, dentures, hearing aids, glasses, incontinence, money, relationships, foster home providers, and transportation. Through "services triage" the occupational therapist has gained a broad knowledge base which has been necessary to accurately assess the timing and depth of intervention. As might be anticipated, some veterans and their caregivers have daily recurrent problems, others never voice a complaint. Thus, at times no news is not necessarily good news and the case manager must be aware of this possibility as well. All that may be needed is reassurance and reminders concerning the process of renewing medications or the doctor or nurse practitioner may need to be alerted about a problem. All real dilemmas are relayed immediately.

The Portland Veterans Administration Hospital is located on two sites; the Vancouver Division (Washington) is approximately 14 miles from the Portland Division (Oregon). Thus, the area served is quite large. The case manager must have a working knowledge of what is available for the veteran in both states. Discharge preparation is a team effort in comprehensive treatment planning meetings. The plan is then carried out by the case manager. Resources offered to the veteran may include VA Outpatient Clinic follow-up, social day programs, financial management resources, caregiver respite programs, bath aides and chore service agencies, and illness specific support groups. Thus, given the multiplicity of the veteran's needs, it is not unusual for the discharge plan to be multifaceted and require skilled coordination.

Of all the expanded knowledge and roles of the case manager/

occupational therapist, the greatest pleasure is the personal interaction with the veteran and his family.

CASE STUDY

Mr. G., age 95 and a World War I veteran, is a widower with no children. His primary medical problem is severe congestive heart failure, he also has decreased vision, is very hard of hearing, unstable ambulation and has urinary incontinence. He is however fully alert and oriented. He has a brother who assists him in managing his finances but Mr. G. writes his own checks.

After a long admission in the VA hospital for treatment of pneumonia and a urinary tract infection Mr. G. became so weakened it was necessary for him to relocate from his home of many years into foster care. He was referred by the hospital team to the newly opened ADHC program for health monitoring, endurance building, and to assist him in his transition and adjustment to his new home. This occupational therapist became his case manager.

From the outset Mr. G. complained of the care at his foster home stating the food was not good and other complaints. These problems were actively listened to by the case manager but consultation with the nurse practitioner assured he was not losing weight or adding water weight in the form of pedal edema. Thus, combined with his grumbles at ADHC activities, the home problems were deemed to be minor and probably necessary in his readjustment to foster home living.

Incontinence, aggravated by the "water pill" Lasix was another issue requiring the intervention of the case manager, with assistance and coordination of the team. Final resolution required experimentation with continence techniques and aides as well as phone conversations with the foster care provider concerning the recommended system.

The case manager also maintained communication with Mr. G.'s 88-year-old brother. He has no car and visits by bus on Sundays. He reported moderate satisfaction with the foster care but stated that he had no comparison. Mr. G. was asked about his care but severe hearing loss made ongoing communication challenging and sometimes confusing, even with the use of amplification devices. Writ-

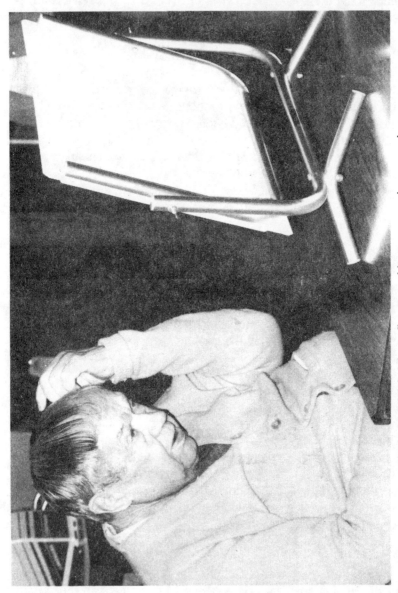

PHOTOGRAPH 2. Ninety-five-year-old veteran practices grooming

ing also proved to be laborious and frequently misunderstood. After approximately two months it became apparent that Mr. G. was not adjusting to his foster home and that indeed some of his complaints were valid. When asked, the brother and the transportation driver reported that at times Mr. G. would be home alone. A visit by the case manager revealed that the home provided inappropriate stimulation and care for Mr. G. and the caregiver frequently left him alone. On the case manager's recommendation, the ADHC team agreed that Mr. G. should move. The case manager then contacted the VA social worker in charge of foster home placement who arranged another home and also dealt with the defective home. The case manager then found a resource in a man with a pick-up truck who moves older people, for a small fee. A case manager/occupational therapist visit to the new home confirmed the success of the move and provided an opportunity to demonstrate safe ambulation techniques and bathroom transfers, issue appropriate equipment, and recommend room rearrangement and lighting changes to optimize Mr. G.'s safe ambulation and optimum care.

Mr. G. is very happy in his new home.

CONCLUSION

Case management of dependent elderly veterans in a day hospital requires therapeutic intervention on many levels and a broad knowledge of community resources. This is now being provided through the Adult Day Health Care Program at the Portland Veterans Administration Medical Center's Vancouver Division. Research will soon be in place to measure its medical efficacy, patient/caregiver satisfaction and cost-effectiveness.

NOTES

1. Corrective Therapy is the applied science of medically prescribed therapeutic exercise, education, and adapted physical activities to improve the quality of life and health of adults and children, by developing physical fitness, increasing functional mobility and independence and improving psychosocial behavior. The Corrective Therapist evaluates, develops, implements and modifies adapted exercise programs for disease, injury, congenital defects and other functional disabilities (Carlson, 1985). Corrective Therapists are employed only in the VA system.

2. The Veterans Administration recognizes employees by FTE (Full-Time Employee). Full-time is designated by 1.0. Any employee working less than full-time is identified by the decimal fraction of the time worked.

3. Veterans who lose earning capacity due to disease or injury incurred in or aggravated during active military service are paid a monthly disability compensation. Disability evaluations range from 10% to 100%, and payments are based on the degree of determined disability.

REFERENCES

Carlson, R. B. (Ed.) (1985). Corrective therapy [Definition]. *American Corrective Therapy Journal, 39*(5), back cover.

Hasselkus, B. (1982). Barthel self-care index and geriatric home care patients. *Physical and Occupational Therapy in Geriatrics, 1*(4), 11-22.

Mahoney, F., & Barthel, D. (1965). Functional evaluation: The Barthel index. *Maryland State Medical Journal, 14*, 61-65.

Ross, M., & Burdick, D. *Sensory Integration.* Thorofare, NJ: SLACK, Inc., 1981.

Veterans Administration (1984). *Caring for the Older Veteran.* Washington, DC: U.S. Government Printing Office.

Veterans Administration (1987). Adult Day Health Care Program Direction/Operating Instructions. Unpublished document compiled by Department of Medicine and Surgery, Veterans Administration, Washington, DC.

Shoe Inserts for Insensitive Feet

Anne Mercier Woodson, OTR

SUMMARY. Peripheral neuropathy is a frequent complication of diabetes. Resulting loss of sensation can lead to the formation of a plantar ulcer which may become infected and ultimately result in amputation of a toe, a foot, or a leg. This sequence of events threatens the patient's independence. Prevention of foot lesions can help to maintain the diabetic's independence as well as reduce the cost of medical care.

An intervention program for the insensitive foot includes patient education, foot evaluation, fabrication of accommodative orthoses to distribute pressure thereby preventing pressure lesions and promoting healing of ulcers already formed.

Foot discomfort is a common complaint of the elderly. In contrast, insensitive or hyposensitive feet are an infrequent patient complaint, yet can lead to serious medical complications resulting in functional impairment. Those with diabetes, peripheral vascular disease or other conditions leading to peripheral neuropathy risk losing sensibility and muscle tone in the feet. Anesthesia deprives the patient of protective sensation by which one normally identifies mechanical stress which could cause tissue destruction (Brand, 1982). In addition, weakness of intrinsic muscles can lead to joint imbalance, prominent metatarsal heads and abnormal concentrations of pressure over the plantar surface which accelerates tissue

Anne Mercier Woodson is Supervisor of Adult Physical Disability Out Patient Occupational Therapy Services of the University of Texas Medical Branch, Galveston, TX 77550.

Appreciation is extended to J. Mark Bruyn, DPM, for his encouragement and guidance in this program, to Dianna Puccetti, OTR, for photography, and to Lillian Hoyle Parent, MA, OTR, for editorial assistance.

33

degeneration (Wyngaarden, 1985). Sensory loss is usually accompanied by a sympathetic nerve dysfunction leading to dry cracking skin which creates further vulnerability.

Repeated undetected mechanical stress can first cause a general weakening of tissue (trophic changes) (Brand, 1982) then callouses and ulceration (Photograph 1). If ulcers are painless, probably they will be neglected and may become infected or gangrenous and may lead ultimately to amputation of a toe, a foot, or a leg. This complication results in increased hospitalization and medical costs, as well as leading to probable reduction in independence. Prevention and early treatment of foot lesions would, therefore, be important measures to maintain independence and reduce the cost of medical care for those individuals at risk.

For the past two years, the Occupational Therapy Clinic in the Ambulatory Care Center at the University of Texas Medical Branch has been involved in an intervention program for patients with insensitive feet in collaboration with the Department of Podiatry. The

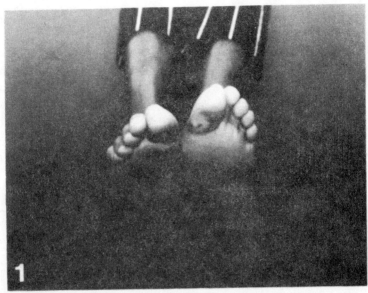

PHOTOGRAPH 1. Trophic ulcers on great toes of patient with longstanding diabetic peripheral neuropathy

program consists of patient education, foot evaluation and provision of foot orthoses. These devices are custom-molded shoe inserts designed to protect the insensitive foot, improve pressure distribution over the plantar surface, prevent high pressure areas and promote healing of existing lesions.

The clinic is part of a large state referral center, serving many patients who live in remote areas. Patients must be scheduled for treatment as soon as they are referred and usually cannot be followed with consistency. Many referrals are "one time" patients, thus treatment must be focused on quick provision of that which will be most useful to the patient and for which the patient or family can assume responsibility.

Occupational Therapy services were solicited by the Department of Podiatry because it was felt that the therapists' skills and resources could be used to provide easily fabricated, inexpensive shoe inserts for patients who had neither the time nor the finances for the more sophisticated type of orthoses produced by podiatry laboratories or an orthotist. Often these inserts may be used on a trial basis to determine effectiveness of orthotics for patients who would then be able to purchase more expensive, longer lasting inserts.

Most patients referred for these services are aged 60 or over; the majority have insulin-dependent diabetes. All have had existing callouses or other lesions for which they sought podiatry services. This population confirms the observation that at least half of all individuals who suffer neurotrophic ulceration develop at least one lesion before they are aware of their sensory loss (Brand, 1982).

RATIONALE FOR SHOE INSERTS

Standing, walking, running or any other weight-bearing activities create low to moderate amounts of mechanical stress to the feet. In the individual with normal feet, repetitive stress such as walking long distances, would eventually cause a mild inflammatory response which seems to make the plantar tissue more fragile than usual (Brand, 1982). If extended walking continues, the individual would feel distinct foot pain and might notice blisters or callouses. Some patients compensate by limping which would serve to reduce stress to regions of the foot receiving the most intense pressure.

Others might sit down to avoid walking altogether. Sensory cues thus serve as natural protection against serious tissue breakdown. An individual with insensitive feet also would experience the same amount and type of mechanical stress walking the same distance. That person does not, however, experience discomfort and may continue hiking without postural adjustment or rest until necrosis and ulceration occur (Brand, 1982). The patient may then be surprised to discover an ulcer and attribute it entirely to the underlying disease process without acknowledging that one has control over the prevention or correction of the problem.

Shoe inserts can serve not only to cushion the stress of ambulation but can also aid in more even distribution of pressure on the plantar surface of the foot to avoid focusing excessive pressure on small areas such as the metatarsal heads or heel. Inserts can do this if they are accommodative, contoured directly to the curves of an individual's plantar surface. This provides greater surface support and distributes pressure more evenly.

The inserts made in this clinic are directly formed to the patient's feet and inserted in appropriate, well-fitting shoes. They can be quickly fabricated (approximately 20 minutes for a pair) with equipment found in most occupational therapy clinics. The material costs are inexpensive (approximately $2.35 a pair).

PATIENT EDUCATION

Therapists and physicians should explain the effects of reduced foot sensibility to the patient. It must be emphasized that this is (usually) a chronic condition and that the patient must learn proper foot care and responsibility or risk serious complications including amputation. Many patients, when questioned, will admit to experiences demonstrating the loss of sensation in their feet. One woman, for example, reported discovering at the end of the day a nail which had punctured her shoe and foot; she was aware of it only when she removed her shoe. A man related that because his feet always "felt cold" (a frequent complaint of this population) he would soak them in hot water to warm them. One day he did this and discovered after several minutes that his skin was blistered and had actually been scalded. Frequently these patients also have reduced sensitivity in their hands and therefore cannot rely on finger touch for valid temperature information. Helping a patient find sensitive parts of their bodies (wrists, elbows) or advising use of thermometers or another person to assist with proper water temperature is an important safety feature.

Careful visual inspection of the feet is another element in foot care. Mirrors or assistance of another person may be necessary if limitation of joint movement is a problem. The patient should be taught to recognize signs of early inflammation and should understand the importance of methods reducing stress to damaged areas. When visual impairment is present, in addition to relying on the assistance of others, adaptations such as large print thermometers or magnifying glasses may be used for foot protection and care.

Other aspects of foot hygiene should be reinforced, including use of appropriate socks or stockings and skin and nail care. Patients should avoid going barefoot, walking on pebbles or other debris inside their shoes, and using home remedy pads or dressings inside shoes. A useful brochure for patient information is "Foot Care for the Diabetic" (Department of Health, Education and Welfare).

Improper shoe selection is a frequent problem. In this clinic most patients have shoes smaller than their feet as evidenced by the fact that an insert which is custom-made to fit a foot is often larger than the shoe. Many patients will insist on wearing stylish but ill-fitting shoes, while others wear predominantly open-toed house shoes which are comfortable but offer little protection for the vulnerable plantar surface of insensitive feet.

MATERIALS AND EQUIPMENT NEEDED

— Alimold (3/8-inch thick) or other closed cell thermoplastic material*
— Gauze (4 x 4s) or similar padding material
— Porous or paper tape
— Rubber foam block approximately 3 x 8 x 14 inches
— Stockinette or thin socks

---

*Alimed, Inc., 68 Harrison Avenue, Boston, MA 02111 is a comprehensive source for insert material.

— Scissors suitable for cutting thermoplastic material
— Oven
— Grinder with drum sander (3-inch diameter with 3-inch face)
with medium grade sandpaper sleeve

EVALUATION

Examine the bare feet for callouses and attempt to elicit reports of numbness. Pinprick evaluation may be performed to determine presence and degree of hyposensitivity. Assess temperature discrimination to educate patients regarding precautionary techniques. Inquire about the amount and type of weight-bearing activity. For example, how much weight-bearing is done daily, on what types of surfaces, how much walking is done, and the type of shoes usually worn.

FABRICATION PROCEDURE

Preheat oven to 325 degrees Fahrenheit (170 degrees Celsius). With patient weight-bearing in usual, comfortable position, trace outlines of bare feet onto Alimold. Although manufacturers do not describe shrinkage in soft thermoplastic materials, the writer has observed that slight shrinkage does occur. The outline of the foot should therefore be traced slightly larger than the foot. It is important to make inserts for both feet even if the patient has lesions of only one foot; this prevents discrepancy in shoe height. Cut inserts with scissors. Pad ulcerated areas on patient's feet using gauze and surgical tape (enough layers to form ¼-inch thickness) (Photograph 2). The padding creates an impression when the Alimold is molded to the foot so that the finished insert will provide reduced pressure to the ulcerated areas. Place one insert in the preheated oven. Inserts can be placed directly on the oven rack or on a flat surface, such as a cookie sheet. Heat for two to three minutes until the insert feels soft and springy. Alimold will smoke and scorch if left in an oven too long, or if oven temperature is too hot.

To mold the insert on the foot, place insert fabric side up on foam block placed on floor aligned under patient's foot. Have patient bear weight evenly on insert for one minute (Photograph 3). Manu-

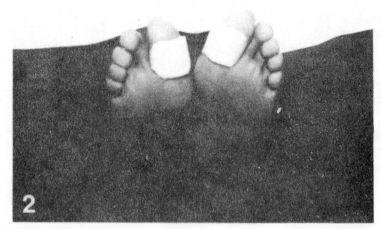

PHOTOGRAPH 2. Temporary padding used to create increased depression on inserts under ulcers

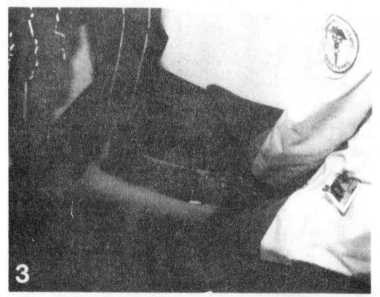

PHOTOGRAPH 3. Molding insert directly to the foot

facturers state that soft insert material can be molded directly to the skin, providing optimum shaping of the inserts. Test temperature of Alimold on your wrist before applying it to the foot. The material should feel warm, but not uncomfortable. If a therapist feels that a patient's skin is particularly fragile and should be protected during the molding process, stockinette or thin socks can be worn by the patient without adverse effects on the shaping of the insert. Be sure to provide support to help patient maintain balance. Adjust position of the foot to center on insert. Repeat the heating and molding process for the second insert.

Grind the inserts on drum sander for better fit in shoe (Photograph 4). Bevel the edges and flatten the metatarsal head and heel areas slightly to prevent the insert from rocking in shoe. Grind the bottom surface only. Place inserts inside shoes (Photograph 5) and have patient don the shoes and walk. Make adjustments as necessary to the inserts. The patient should wear sturdy comfortable shoes with sufficient depth in the toe area to avoid excessive pressure over the dorsum. Shoes should be one half to one size larger

PHOTOGRAPH 4. Finishing inserts on grinder

PHOTOGRAPH 5. Fitting inserts into shoes

than the size regularly worn to accommodate extra bulk of insert. The padding placed in the shoe by the manufacturer can sometimes be removed to provide necessary room. Patients should periodically have inserts replaced as they compress. Follow-up of the patient is encouraged to check for proper fit and use of inserts and to monitor areas of pressure.

DISCUSSION

Custom-molded accommodative shoe inserts for the patient with insensitive or hyposensitive feet are used to promote independence in ambulatory activities. Short term goals include provision of a protective surface for insensitive feet; improvement of pressure distribution over the plantar surface to reduce the forces of weight bearing; promotion of healing for existing trophic lesions; and prevention of recurrence or development of new lesions.

Though consistent follow-up of these patients has been difficult because of the large number who live out of town, most patients who have returned have reported favorable reactions to use of the inserts. They claim daily use of the inserts, increased comfort and well-being of their feet, gradual healing of ulcers and no new development of foot lesions. Additional research on the use of orthoses is necessary to determine the effectiveness of this treatment for long term preservation of the insensitive foot. These services should be expanded to serve the population at risk earlier, before the development of lesions, to be a true prevention program.

REFERENCES

Brand, P.W. (1982). "The Insensitive Foot". In M. Jahss (Ed.), *Disorders of the Foot*, Vol. 2. Philadelphia: W.B. Saunders Company.

Wyngaarden, J.B. & Smith, L.H. (Eds.) (1985). *Cecil's Textbook of Medicine* (17th ed.), Vol. 2. Philadelphia: W.B. Saunders Company.

BIBLIOGRAPHY

Bauman, J.H. & Brand, P.W. (1963). Measurement of Pressure Between Foot and Shoe. *Lancet*, 629-632.

Boulton, A.J., Franks, C.I. et al. (1984). Reduction of Abnormal Foot Pressures in Diabetic Neuropathy Using a New Polymer Insole Material. *Diabetes Care*, 7(1), January-February, 42-46.

Brand, P.W. & Ebner, J.D. (1969). A Pain Substitute Pressure Assessment for the Insensitive Limb. *The American Journal of Occupational Therapy*, 23(6), November-December, 479-486.

Brand, P.W. & Ebner, J.D. (1969). Pressure Sensitive Devices for Denervated Hands and Feet. *Journal of Bone and Joint Surgery*, 51-A(1), January, 109-116.

Brenner, M.A. (1974). An Ambulatory Approach to the Neuropathic Ulceration. *Journal American Podiatry Association*, 64(11), November, 862-866.

Robson, M.C. & Edstrom, L.E. (1977). The Diabetic Foot: An Alternative Approach to Major Amputation. *Surgical Clinics of North America*, 57(5), October, 1089-1102.

Sensory Stimulation
and ADL Performance:
A Single Case Study Approach

Carol A. Smith, OT

SUMMARY. This study examined the effect of sensory stimulation on ADL performance in an elderly individual with diabetes mellitus. A single subject study was conducted, employing an A-B, multiple baseline, across behaviors design. The subject was a 65-year-old woman with diabetes mellitus and multiple sensory deficits as a result of complications of her disease. After two weeks of baseline data, the subject participated in 30-minute sensory stimulation sessions, three times a week for four weeks. A shirt buttoning and phone book task were measured for both speed and accuracy and an insulin administration task for accuracy alone. Performance was measured before and after each session to examine the cumulative and immediate arousal effects. Analysis with the C-statistic revealed a significant time reduction on the shirt buttoning task at the $p <$ .001 level. Visual analysis illustrated reduction in time in both the shirt buttoning and phone book tasks. Results indicate that sensory stimulation can have a direct effect on functional performance.

An estimated 25% of all individuals over age 85 have diabetes mellitus (Rowe & Besdine, 1982) as compared to approximately 1% in the 18-44 age group (U.S. Bureau of the Census, 1985). A number of factors account for the apparent increase in diabetes with

---

The author wishes to thank Ron Stone, MS, OTR/L, Juli Evans, MS, OTR/L, and Steve Morelan, PhD, OTR/L, of the University of Puget Sound, School of Occupational and Physical Therapy for their assistance in designing this study and in preparing the manuscript, and Joy Cunningham for sharing her time and first-hand knowledge. This paper was written in partial fulfillment of the requirements for the degree of Master of Occupational Therapy from the University of Puget Sound.

age: obesity, extended life-span, and increased screening in the elderly. Long life is accompanied by a normal decrease in carbohydrate tolerance, precipitating diabetes in individuals with an inherited predisposition (Rowe & Besdine, 1982).

Degeneration occurs in the senses with age in a linear fashion, with the greatest changes occurring from middle age onward. These changes are a result of anatomical and neurological changes in the sensory systems. In the 75-79 year age group 75% have hearing impairments and only 15 out of 100 people have 20/20 vision, even with vision corrected (Ernst & Glazer-Waldman, 1983). Evidence suggests that changes occur in the tactile, vestibular, proprioceptive, gustatory, and olfactory systems as well (Colavita, 1978; Ernst & Glazer-Waldman, 1983; Kenshalo, 1979; Schiffman, Orlandi, & Erickson, 1979). "Decline in sensory and perceptual functions with age results in less input of environmental information and increasing probability of less than optimum performance by the elderly" (Han & Geha-Mitzel, 1979, p. 311).

Elderly individuals with diabetes mellitus experience magnified sensory deficits. Diabetic retinopathy and neuropathy are frequent long-term complications of the disease. These conditions result in losses in the visual and tactile senses respectively. Vestibular and auditory dysfunctions have also been noted secondary to diabetes. Occupational therapists should be aware of diabetic complications when designing treatment programs.

Limitations in sensory input can affect safety, functional ability, self-image, and interaction with others. Since sensory threshold levels increase with age, stronger stimuli are required to activate the receptors (Lewis, 1985). "Sensory stimulation is designed to produce an adaptive response, which is defined as behavior of a more advanced, organized, flexible, or productive nature" (Farber, 1982, p. 120). The purpose of this study was to examine whether an individual sensory stimulation program would improve the ADL performance of an elderly individual with diabetes mellitus.

REVIEW OF THE LITERATURE

A variety of experimental studies, according to Zubek (1969), have been conducted to examine the effects of controlled sensory and perceptual deprivation on performance. Behaviors reported include hallucinations, visual sensations, reduced cognitive performance, and a greater susceptibility to external influence or persuasion. Clear evidence supports that both simple and complex visual motor coordination are negatively influenced by sensory and perceptual deprivation, with long durations of social isolation alone producing the same effect. In a study of two-week perceptual deprivation Zubek observed motivational losses "such as inability to study or engage in purposeful activity" (p. 61).

Weinberg and Lindsley (1964) illustrated that the starting or stopping of a stimulus can elicit electroencephalographic and behavioral arousal. They surmised that change in the level of stimulation can change the adaptation level of the reticular formation. One of the main functions of the reticular system is arousal which includes signaling the human being to be alert and to attend (Schultz, 1965).

The reticular system is thought to receive input from sensory stimulation and cortical impulses. Cortical stimulation interacting with sensory influences in the reticular system is said to affect the action of the reticular activating system upon the cortex. Thus, both interoceptive and exteroceptive stimuli affect arousal state, determining an individual's capacity for efficient behavior (Schultz, 1965).

Schultz (1965) stated that "an optimal level of cortical arousal is thus considered necessary for efficient adaptive behavior to occur" (p. 18). The absence of adequate external stimulation can decrease arousal effects of cortically produced stimuli (Schultz, 1965). Sensory stimulation therapy is thus an attempt to increase the exteroceptive or sensory input in individuals experiencing reduction.

Richman (1969) developed a sensory training program for a geriatric elderly population with severe psychomotor retardation. "The goal of sensory training is to increase sensitivity and discrimination of feelings through stimulation of all sense receptors" (Richman, 1969, p. 256). Richman (1969) reported clinical evidence of increased levels of functioning in the patients involved in sensory training. Although designed for a group, Lewis implied that Richman's technique can successfully be employed for individual treatment (Lewis, 1979).

Paire and Karney (1984) conducted an experimental study on the effectiveness of sensory stimulation with 30 geropsychiatric inpatients, applying the principles advocated by Richman. Performance was measured in the areas of orientation, self-care skills and inter-personal skills. Significant increases were found in caring for personal hygiene needs and in participation in group activities with continued improvements noted on a six-week follow-up evaluation.

Geriatric patients have been presumed to experience environmental deprivation as a result of their institutionalization. Little consideration has been given to the noninstitutionalized elderly in this regard. Erber (1979) suggests that the degree of social stimulation available to the elderly be evaluated. Individuals living alone in a senior citizens apartment building may receive less stimulation than those in institutions. In any case, this issue has been relatively unexplored.

In discussing sensory retraining therapy Erber (1979) recommended that "careful evaluation of its effects on various types of geriatric patients . . . would increase our knowledge about how to deal optimally with the institutionalized geriatric patient" (p. 175). Elderly persons with diabetes mellitus receive limited sensory input by virtue of the aging process and complications of their disease, and therefore appear to be likely candidates for sensory stimulation treatment.

Diabetic retinopathy is now the leading cause of new blindness in the United States (Podolsky & Schachar, 1979; Rowe & Besdine, 1982). Maturity onset diabetes is often first recognized during a visit to an eye doctor due to vision problems such as blurred vision or total blindness. Diabetic retinopathy is an added detriment in the elderly who may already be suffering some age-related vision loss (Rowe & Besdine, 1982).

Polyneuropathy, the most common form of neuropathy associated with diabetes "refers to loss of nerve function that occurs most notably in the distal branches of many nerve trunks as they enter the hands and feet" (Schaumburg, Spencer, & Thomas, 1983). The sensory deficit first appears as numbing, tingling, and burning sensations, most severe in the feet. A neurological exam shows decrease or absence of touch, pain, temperature, vibration, and position sensations in distal portions of the extremities (Sumner, 1980).

Vestibular and auditory dysfunction are common in the elderly population with diabetes mellitus. Vestibular symptoms include chronic disequilibrium and dizziness. Auditory degeneration is manifested as progressive bilateral high frequency hearing loss. These conditions are attributed to the vascular changes that occur with diabetes (Bahloh & Honrubia, 1979).

/ The elderly person with diabetes may have increased self-care requirements. Special attention must be paid to hygiene with regular inspection for skin infections or lesions on all parts of the body (Blevins, 1979). Food preparation requires greater thought and planning to follow special dietary guidelines. Insulin often needs to be self-administered. Urine and blood sugar must be tested. Such tasks of diabetic management are often difficult for elderly individuals.

King (1978) emphasizes "the fact that 'eliciting an adaptive response'. . . is, in essence, eliciting goal-directed or purposeful behavior" (p. 434). Sensory stimulation has been shown to increase the level of functioning in geropsychiatric populations (Paire & Karney, 1984; Richman, 1969). This type of therapy is worthy of exploration as a tool to enhance performance in elderly individuals with diabetes mellitus.

METHODOLOGY

The study conducted here was of a single subject, employing an A-B, multiple baseline, across behaviors design. The subject was a 65-year-old woman who had been diagnosed with diabetes mellitus in 1943 and lived independently in her own home. Her vision was impaired and she had limited senses of smell and taste. Diabetic neuropathy had effected numbness in her hands, legs, and feet. Although not diagnosed, the subject appeared to have some vestibular deficit, which was reflected in poor balance and occasional dizziness upon exercise.

After baseline data was collected for two weeks, the subject participated in sensory stimulation sessions three times a week for four weeks. The sensory stimulation program lasted approximately 30 minutes and consisted of the systematic focusing of attention on the senses in the order that follows: vestibular, proprioceptive, tactile, olfactory, visual, auditory, and gustatory. Although not used by Richman, vestibular input was included based on Ayre's characterization of its influence on all other concurrent sensations (Ayres,

1972). The subject was given the opportunity to react to each stimulus. Sessions became progressively more difficult, with the beginning sessions addressing identification of objects and the latter sessions requiring more discrimination. Treatment was based on the following principles and guidelines.

Vestibular

Sessions began with vestibular input, because it is the first sensory system to develop and modulates the perception of visual, tactile, and proprioceptive input. Early sessions of simple rocking or head rolling progressed to more varied movements in later sessions. Vestibular input is assumed to lead to more accurate orientation of the body in space, hence better body scheme and motor skills (Ayres, 1985; Ayres, 1972).

Proprioceptive

Body part identification was used in early sessions to focus on proprioceptive input. Imitation of postures and weight bearing were used in later sessions. Proprioceptive input is believed to facilitate body percept, motor planning and stability (Ayres, 1985; Stockmeyer, 1967).

Tactile

Objects with a variety of textures were offered for the subject to identify in early sessions and in later sessions to discriminate. Tactile input is thought to encourage the ability to localize and discriminate touch, effecting accurate body percept, motor planning, and skilled movement (Ayres, 1985; Stockmeyer, 1967).

Olfactory

Due to its connections with the limbic system the olfactory system is believed to have a strong influence on feeding behavior, the enjoyment of food, and long term memory storage. The subject was asked to identify and discriminate food odors and was encouraged to relate any associations (Colavita, 1978; Farber, 1982).

Visual

Shape and color identification in early sessions graduating to discrimination in later sessions were used to promote visual space and form perception and environmental awareness (Ayres, 1985; Colavita, 1978).

Auditory

Stimulation included use of a variety of musical tapes. The subject identified sounds in the beginning and recognized differences in later sessions. Such auditory input is believed to refine auditory adaptive responses, improving speech comprehension and production and ability to approximate the location of a sound source, an important survival mechanism (Ayres, 1985; Colavita, 1978; Farber, 1982).

Gustatory

Gustatory stimulation was provided at the end of each session as reinforcement, because taste nerve fibers connect with the division of the limbic system affecting motivation (Colavita, 1978). Early sessions used familiar foods and strongly opposing flavors. Later sessions required more subtle discriminations. This type of gustatory exercise is assumed to lead to better taste perception and enjoyment of food.

Because the subject's auditory sense was strong, musical tapes were played at each session to maximize the use of her best sense. She was asked to identify and discriminate styles of music, different performers, and a variety of musical instruments. Her musical preferences were taken into consideration when choosing the tapes.

Although the subject appeared to experience no sensation of smell, olfactory stimulation was maintained in the program for the benefit of prompting associations and memory of experiences. Even though she did not smell the odors, after the researcher identified the stimulus she often described the smell as she remembered it and recalled events in her past.

The subject's gustatory sense was quite limited as well. For this reason foods were chosen for their distinct textures along with their flavors. Often the patient identified the food by its tactile qualities rather than its taste.

The work of Ross and Burdick (1981) was used as a basis for vestibular and proprioceptive stimulation. Suggestions for exercise and movement for the elderly were adapted to provide the appropriate sensory stimulation. Sessions were conducted with the subject seated on days when she was feeling less well.

The subject's performance was measured on three ADL tasks, prior to and following each intervention session, for the purpose of recording both the cumulative effects of treatment, and the arousal effects immediately after a session. Target behaviors and measures were as follows:

Shirt Buttoning. The task consisted of buttoning nine buttons on the same shirt. Speed was measured as the length of time in seconds required to complete nine buttons.

Phone Book. The task required looking up a prescribed number in the yellow pages and writing it down in a notebook. Measures included the length of time in seconds to complete the task and the number of errors incurred when recording the phone number.

Insulin Administration. The task was comprised of filling a syringe with two types of insulin. Accuracy was measured in terms of the number of units off from the required dosage and the number of air bubbles in the syringe.

RESULTS

The speed of the shirt buttoning task was analyzed using the C-statistic and comparison of the baseline and cumulative measure (taken prior to each session) yielded a statistically significant reduction in the amount of time required to complete the buttoning task, $z = 2.86, p < .001$. The C-statistic was used for its ability to quantitatively support trends recognized in visual analysis. Analysis of baseline and arousal measure (taken after each session) also yielded a significant reduction in time, $z = 2.43, p < .001$. Visual analysis was consistent with the C-statistic in demonstrating a change in level from baseline for both the cumulative and arousal measures (see Figure 1). Difference between cumulative and arousal mea-

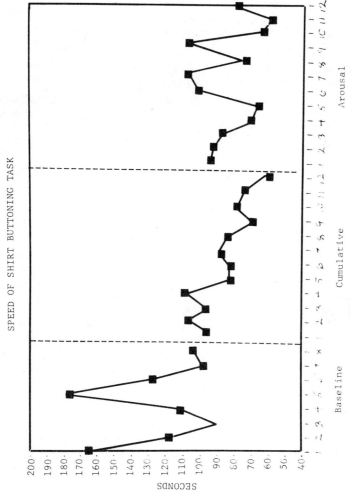

FIGURE 1. Time required to complete shirt buttoning task during baseline and before (cumulative) and after (arousal) each intervention

51

sures was examined for the immediate arousal effects, but no significant differences were found, statistically or through visual analysis.

Speed on the phone book task was analyzed with the C-statistic. There was a reduction in time between baseline and cumulative measure but it failed to reach statistical significance. Visual analysis illustrated this drop in scores (see Figure 2). Analysis of differences between baseline and arousal measure and cumulative and arousal measures revealed no statistical significance.

Accuracy measures on the phone book task and insulin administration revealed minimal errors so that the data did not lend itself to visual or statistical analysis.

DISCUSSION AND CONCLUSION

The performance on the shirt buttoning task clearly demonstrated a gain which seems to be associated with the sensory stimulation intervention. This was consistent with the findings of Paire and Karney (1984), empirically supporting the assumption that sensory stimulation has a direct effect on functional performance. Because promoting function is one of the central premises of occupational therapy, such verification is a significant finding for the profession.

An explanation for the reduction in time required to complete the shirt buttoning task could be that vestibular, proprioceptive, and tactile input are all thought to contribute to motor skill. In addition, these are the first sensory systems to develop and believed by Ayres to have the most far-reaching effects on performance. Stimulation of these sensory channels may have reflected in enhanced performance on the shirt buttoning task.

The absence of a difference in the speed of the phone book task across time may have been due to some inherent inconsistency of the task itself. Although phone numbers were preselected, the task was not uniformly difficult. Each page of the phone book yellow pages is displayed differently, making some numbers easier to find than others. A modification of this task to provide for more controls might result in less variability.

Another factor that may have accounted for the lack of statistical

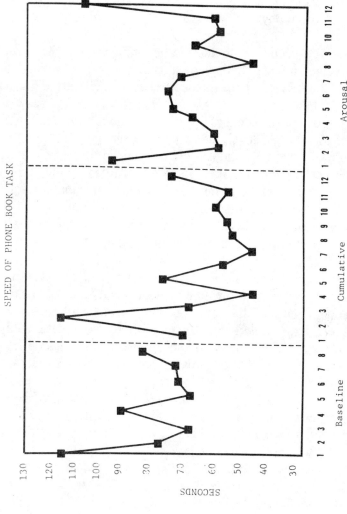

FIGURE 2. Time required to complete phone book task during baseline and before (cumulative) and after (arousal) each intervention

53

significance was the variability of scores for the phone book task. Although the shirt buttoning and the phone book tasks both required vision and motor coordination, the phone book task had a greater visual component. The subject's functional vision appeared to vary significantly from day to day, associated with differences in blood sugar level.

Measures of speed on both the shirt buttoning and the phone book tasks illustrated a wide variance in scores. Many factors may have influenced the subject's performance and accounted for the fluctuation in scores from session to session. These include the subject's variable vision, inconsistent peripheral sensation, arthritis, angina, control of blood sugar level, and brief illnesses.

Measure of short term arousal effects yielded no significant reduction in performance time on either task. Perhaps having to perform the same task twice in one session hindered improvement in performance due to factors such as boredom, frustration, and the repetitious nature of the tasks. A more sensitive measure may have been necessary to examine the immediate effects of sensory stimulation.

In spite of medical limitations, the subject of this study functioned at a high level. She lived independently and did her own homemaking. She had developed techniques of compensation for some of her sensory deficits. A similar study conducted with a lower functioning, less motivated subject may have yielded more dramatic changes. In addition, this subject was only 65 years old. An older individual might have incurred a greater loss of sensory receptors by virtue of his or her advanced age. It is conceivable that such a subject would have provided lower baseline scores and a greater potential for an improved response to stimulus.

Several limitations were contained in this single subject investigation. The effectiveness of sensory stimulation for the subject of this study cannot be generalized to the diabetic elderly population with confidence. This subject possessed a unique set of sensory deficits which will not occur identically in other individuals with the same diagnosis. The study's A-B design provided no measure of carry-over effects of the intervention. Finally, the 4-week length of the intervention measured only the effectiveness of a short term sensory stimulation program.

In conclusion, this preliminary study revealed the following: sensory stimulation had a positive effect on speed of performance on selected functional tasks with one elderly individual with diabetes mellitus. Time reduction for the shirt buttoning task was statistically significant and visual analysis reflected a drop in scores for the phone book task, thus supporting the effectiveness of sensory stimulation in improving ADL performance. Such evidence verifies the worth of further investigation of this technique for the treatment of elderly individuals with diabetes mellitus.

This study introduced the efficacy of utilizing sensory stimulation with this population. Continued investigations employing both experimental and single subject designs would expand our base of knowledge in this area. Future studies would be strengthened by incorporating the daily monitoring of subject blood sugar level. This would allow for statistical analysis to determine correlations between performance and level of blood glucose. Such information would provide added insight into the value of a sensory stimulation intervention.

Perhaps sensory stimulation therapy can be incorporated early with the at-risk elderly to prevent decreases in function. Mental and physical health may be maintained if attention is paid to the sensory environment. Too often this aspect is ignored until an individual exhibits subnormal behaviors. If populations in need are identified, supplementary sensory input can be provided within the context of preventative health-care programs. Individuals who are at risk of sensory deprivation may be treated with foresight rather than hindsight.

REFERENCES

Ayres, A. J. (1972). *Sensory Integration and Learning Disorders*. Los Angeles: Western Psychological Services.

Ayres, A. J. (1985). *Sensory Integration and the Child*. Los Angeles: Western Psychological Services.

Bahloh, R. W., Honrubia, V. (1979). *Clinical Neurophysiology of the Vestibular System*. Philadelphia: F. A. Davis Company.

Blevins, D. R. (1979). *The Diabetic and Nursing Care*. New York: McGraw-Hill Book Co.

Colavita, F. B. (1978). *Sensory Changes in the Elderly*. Springfield, IL: Charles C Thomas.

Erber, J. T. (1979). The institutionalized geriatric patient considered in a framework of developmental deprivation. *Human Development, 122*, 165-179.

Ernst, N. S., & Glazer-Waldman, H. R. (1983). *The Aged Patient*. Chicago: Year Book Publishers, Inc.

Farber, S. D. (1982). *Neurorehabilitation, A Multisensory Approach*. Philadelphia: W. B. Saunders Company.

Han, S. S., & Geha-Mitzel, M. (1979). Coping with Sensory Losses in Aging. In J. M. Ordy & K. R. Brizee (Eds.), *Sensory Systems and Communication in the Elderly* (pp. 311-315). New York: Raven Press.

Kenshalo, D. R. (1979). Changes in the Vestibular and Somesthetic Systems as a Function of Age. In J. M. Ordy & K. R. Brizee (Eds.), *Sensory Systems and Communication in the Elderly* (pp. 269-282). New York: Raven Press.

King, L. J. (1978). Towards a science of adaptive responses. *American Journal of Occupational Therapy, 32*, 429-437.

Lewis, C. B. (1985). *Aging: The Health Care Challenge*. Philadelphia: F. A. Davis Company.

Lewis, S. C. (1979). *The Mature Years: A Geriatric Occupational Therapy Text*. Thorofare, NJ: Charles B. Black, Inc.

Paire, A., & Karney, R. J. (1984). The effectiveness of sensory stimulation for geropsychiatric inpatients. *American Journal of Occupational Therapy, 22*, 165-179.

Podolsky, S., & Schachar, R. A. (1979). Clinical Manifestations of Diabetic Retinopathy and Other Diseases of the Eye in the Elderly. In J. M. Ordy & K. R. Brizee (Eds.), *Sensory Systems and Communication in the Elderly* (pp. 61-83). New York: Raven Press.

Richman, L. (1969). Sensory training for geriatric patients. *American Journal of Occupational Therapy, 123*, 254-256.

Ross, M., & Burdick, D. (1981). *Sensory Integration, A Training Manual for Therapists and Teachers for Regressed, Psychiatric and Geriatric Patient Groups*. Thorofare, NJ: SLACK, Incorporated.

Rowe, J. W., & Besdine, R. W. (Eds.) (1982). *Health and Disease in Old Age*. Boston: Little, Brown, and Company.

Schaumburg, H. H., Spencer, P. S., & Thomas, P. K. (1983). *Disorders of Peripheral Nerves*. Philadelphia: F. A. Davis Company.

Schiffman, S., Orlandi, M., & Erickson, R. P. (1979). Changes in Taste and Smell with Age: Biological Aspects. In J. M. Ordy & K. R. Brizee (Eds.), *Sensory Systems and Communication in the Elderly* (pp. 247-268). New York: Raven Press.

Schultz, D. P. (1965). *Sensory Restriction, Effects on Behavior*. New York: Academic Press.

Stockmeyer, S. A. (1967). An interpretation of the approach of Rood to the treatment of neuromuscular dysfunction. *American Journal of Physical Medicine, 146,* 900-942.

Sumner, A. J. (1980). *The Physiology of Peripheral Nerve Disease.* Philadelphia: W. B. Saunders Company.

U. S. Bureau of the Census. (1985). *Statistical Abstract of the United States: 1986* (106th ed.). Washington, DC: Author.

Weinberg, N., & Lindsley, D. (1964). Behavioral and EEG arousal to contrasting novel stimulation. *Science, 144,* 1355-1357.

Zubek, J. P. (Ed.) (1969). *Sensory Deprivation: Fifteen Years of Research.* New York: Appleton-Century-Crofts.

Sexuality and Aging:
A Community Wellness Program

Linda Fazio, PhD, OTR

SUMMARY. Community programs serving the elderly are becoming actively involved in the support of comprehensive wellness to meet the changing needs of the aging adult. An occupational therapy perspective enjoys compatibility with community wellness programs by recognizing the community as an arena for practice and by encouraging a broad view of wellness to include many occupational roles for the aging adult. This paper addresses the expression of sexuality as a component of occupational behavior through a description of a program designed to assist the aging adult to (1) become more aware of the processes of normal sexual development, (2) become more aware of changes that are likely to occur in sexual needs and functions with aging, (3) understand the impact of illness, disability and medications on sexual functioning, and (4) view sexuality within one's occupational profile.

INTRODUCTION

Community programs serving the elderly such as senior centers, recreation and leisure components of city parks and recreation, retirement villages and churches are becoming actively involved in the support of comprehensive wellness programs to meet the needs of the aging adult. Johnson (1986) strengthens the relationship between wellness and occupational therapy. She describes wellness as a "proactive way of life" (p. 753). She emphasizes balance in a pattern of living to include work, play, rest, and leisure. An occu-

---

Linda Fazio is Assistant Professor of Clinical Occupational Therapy, University of Southern California, 12933 Erickson Avenue, Bldg. 30, Downey, CA 90242.

pational therapy perspective enjoys compatibility with community wellness programs by recognizing the community as an arena for practice and by encouraging a broad view of wellness to include many occupational roles for the aging adult. Roles that may be ignored by other caregivers and by the aging adults themselves.

Occupational behaviors experienced by the aging individual evolve, shift and change over time but the need for an age-appropriate balance between productive behaviors, leisure, and self-care does not change.

Many aging individuals prepare for retirement by anticipating major shifts in occupational roles often to include the abandonment of productive behaviors. Oftentimes new leisure activities are cultivated or old ones revived. Self-care and those associated behaviors facilitating feelings of self-worth, independence and subjective wellness may have less of an emphasis as aging occurs. Health related changes may further disturb independent attention to self-care and daily living skills.

Neglecting a balanced occupational profile at any age, but particularly in later years, may provide the basis for depression and a sense of loss often reported by the elderly.

Sexuality has been recognized as a life skill by occupational therapists for some time (Dahl, 1978). The realm of sexual functioning includes the performance of physical and emotional behaviors that impact on all aspects of the occupational profile. Chipouras et al. (1979) indicates that sexuality is one important way we define and present ourselves to others as people, and as men and women. Neistadt (1986) states that sexuality is an integral part of the human experience. As such sexuality does not cease to exist with age. George and Weiler (1981) speak of the prevalence of myths surrounding sexuality in late adulthood. Their data dispel the myth of the asexual older person; and the prevalence of irreversible impotency in aging males. Their findings seem to indicate that sexual interest and activity remain more stable over middle and late life than previously suggested.

The expression of sexuality as a component of occupational behavior evolves, shifts and changes over time but the need for the inclusion of sexuality in the balance of life does not change.

This paper addresses the life skill of sexuality by offering a description of a specific program designed to help the aging adult become more aware of the processes of normal sexual development and the concomitant changes in sexual needs and functions as aging occurs. Assisting the elderly toward improvements in understanding of sexual functioning is not an end in itself but a means of helping achieve the timeless need for intimacy, trust, affection, and caring.

Secondly the program's design includes those who are working with aging adults to assist them in the process of examining their own social and cultural attitudes and their information regarding sexuality. The recognition of aging as a continuum permits the program to provide relevancy for all attendees.

GOALS OF THE PROGRAM

The program's goals are (1) educational: to gain accurate information on sexuality and aging; (2) attitude adjustment: to gain acceptance and understanding of one's own sexuality and that of others; and (3) awareness: to be more fully cognizant of one's life roles and the ability to alter them if needed. The purpose is to provide accurate information on sexuality for males and females and to offer a supportive and facilitative climate for sharing concerns and questions regarding sexuality and occupational roles.

FORMAT OF THE PROGRAM

A conceptual framework for sexuality counseling developed by Annon (1974) was used as a general approach to the program. The framework is flexible and comprehensive and can be easily adapted to many settings and populations. It is also readily adapted to the comfort level and skills of the program leader. It appears to be as appropriate for groups as it is for individuals (Annon, 1974).

The conceptual model is referred to as the P-LI-SS-IT (PLISSIT) model. The model provides for four levels of approach. The four levels are: *P*ermission-*L*imited *I*nformation-*S*pecific *S*uggestions-*I*ntensive *T*herapy. Each descending level of approach requires increasing degrees of knowledge, training, and skill on the part of the leader or helper. The model allows the individual to gear his approach to his own particular level of comfort and competence.

The first levels of permission and limited information are most appropriate for use by occupational therapists and were found to meet the needs of the community groups in almost all cases.

Most attendees are seeking information and assurance that they are "normal" and that nothing is wrong with them or their spouse. Persons who require more attention than the first two stages of the model provide should be referred to a counselor or therapist prepared to give more intensive therapy.

Several techniques are used to facilitate group response and interaction. The groups have most often been attended by more females than males. When larger numbers of males are in attendance it is often helpful to divide the groups with the assistance of a male coleader. This will vary depending on the socioeconomic, educational level and cultural orientation of the group.

These factors must always be considered carefully when planning programs. The nature of the room, arrangement of chairs, classroom versus social orientations must all meet the expectations of the group.

All programs, regardless of setting, are initiated by an introduction to the leaders and to the format that will be used. The attendees will be more responsive if they have some assurance that the leaders know more than they do about the subject. A classroom format is useful for a portion of each program, followed by small interactive group discussions. Specific factual information includes: (1) an overview of normal sexual functioning from birth to death for the male and the female; (2) changes that may be expected to occur in sexual functioning from middle to later years; and (3) changes in sexual functioning that may be due to illness. The information portion of each program is interspersed with opportunities for questions and more informal anecdotes appropriate to the particular audience. Following each information segment small groups are encouraged to respond by sharing from their own experiences. They are often asked to write down questions for the leaders, or other participants which are then shared anonymously at the next program.

Program format is best expressed in three or more meetings of two to three hours each.

CONTENT OF THE PROGRAM

The following represents an overview of the material provided in the programs. It is not intended to be exhaustive. Factual material is selected based on the present information level and the expressed needs of the groups.

Introduction

Kaplan (1974) relates that the potential for erotic pleasure seems to begin with birth and does not need to end until death. However, age shapes the biologic component of our sexuality so that the intensity and quality of the sexual response varies at different ages. According to Claman (1966) and George and Weiler (1981) the greater sexual interest, activity, and capacity in earlier life, the greater sexual interest, activity, and capacity in later years, which seems to support the concept of continuity of life-style in aging. While prior activity and interest affect later activity both sexes are greatly influenced by the presence or absence of a socially appropriate sexual partner (George and Weiler, 1981).

Kinsey (1953, 1948) and Masters and Johnson's studies (1966) indicate that men experience the peak of sexual responsiveness and capacity around the ages of seventeen and eighteen and thereafter show a steady decline. Women, on the other hand, attain their sexual peak in their late thirties and early forties and thereafter decline at a relatively slower rate than men. The components of sexual response are affected differently by age. Masters and Johnson's studies (1970, 1966) have revealed that the male orgasm is the most vulnerable to the effects of normal aging. The aging male, though, can anticipate experiencing occasional orgasm and can have frequent erections with effective stimulation. Age seems to have no comparable effect on women, who remain capable of multiple orgasms essentially without long lapses in between, throughout life. Providing that health remains good, a couple can enjoy the giving and receiving of sexual pleasure throughout their lives. According to Kaplan (1974) the majority of sexual complaints of the elderly are a product of the couples' lack of awareness of normal age-related biological changes in the sexual response, and the inability to communicate needs and concerns to each other. Age-related physical changes in sexual interest and responsiveness provide potential not only for individual and marital stress, but also for the enhancement of love relationships. Lovemaking techniques can accommodate each partner's changing needs for stimulation and gratification, and the relationship has potential for great enrichment.

Male Sexuality and Aging

By the time the well male reaches forty-plus, the quality of sexual pleasure has often begun to change noticeably from the intense, genitally localized sensations of youth to the more sensuous but diffused and generalized experience characteristic of middle and later life (Kaplan, 1974). After age fifty frequency of male orgasm and the resting period between orgasms change significantly. After age fifty love play may need alterations to fit the need for longer and more intense stimulations to achieve an erection and ejaculation. Very extended periods of love play and stimulation after an erection is achieved may cause the loss of erection without ejaculation for as long as twelve to twenty-four hours. Following ejaculation there is a refractory period when the penis does not respond by erection and it appears to be age related. From one to ten minutes in males below twenty to hours and days in those from fifty to seventy (Newman, 1986).

There is some decline in sexual interest, thoughts and fantasies from about age fifty on except in the case of specific erotic stimulation. Masters and Johnson (1970) reported that many men move from effective sexual functioning to varying levels of secondary impotence as they age, because they don't understand the natural variants that physiological aging imposes on previously established patterns of sexual functioning. If the aging male and/or his partner are prepared for the natural delays in reaction time to sexual stimuli they need not panic and through anxiety experience impotence.

In the total cycle of sexual response, the largest number of physiological changes to come within objective focus for older men occur during the orgasmic phase of the ejaculatory process. The stage of ejaculatory inevitability or the sense of immediacy may be totally missing from the aging male's sexual response cycle; in addition, the seminal fluid volume is reduced as is the expulsive contraction.

However, none of these alterations seems to detract from the aging male's subjective interpretation of pleasure. The resolution phase of the older male's sexual response cycle exhibits a period following ejaculation during which the male is biophysically unresponsive to sexual stimuli. If both the male and his partner understand this there will be no frustration at trying to initiate a second intercourse too quickly. The introduction of new female partners may restore at least a transient erectile response and a shortened refractory period (Newman, 1986).

As the male ages he has much better ejaculatory control than his younger counterpart. At the same time he experiences less of a need to ejaculate only every second or third coital connection and if he does not ejaculate, he can return to erection rapidly after prior loss of an erection through distraction or female satiation.

The older man may experience no difficulty in achieving and maintaining an erection if there is no ejaculatory threat. This threat may often be the uniformed partner who insists he ejaculate. If each partner is permitted, and invited to enjoy sex in the way they wish, satisfying sexual relationships can continue indefinitely. It is important to remember that the aging male may note delayed erective time, a one stage rather than a two stage orgasmic experience, reduction in seminal fluid volume, and decreased ejaculatory pressure, but he does not lose his facility for erection at anytime if he remains in good health (Masters and Johnson, 1970).

For many men, late forties and fifties are years of intense investment in career. Sexual energy and interest may be diverted to work. This may be increasingly true for females as they become more invested in careers. Males and females, however, remain potentially responsive to sexual stimulation throughout life especially if active sexuality and good health have been maintained.

If a male is prepared for the changes that occur in other areas of his life during later years, that is, relinquishing control over his work environment, changes in leisure, he need not experience an exaggerated sense of sexual loss that often accompanies other areas of perceived loss. Some men respond to age related declines in sexual interest and ability by seeking out new partners and new sexual techniques. Other men, by contrast, may cease to have sexual intercourse at all. This abstinence is often a psychological avoidance of frustration, anxiety, and depression that may be elicited by confrontation with their declining sexual performance. Impotence may also be a frequent complaint of this age group. These concerns may be anticipated and when both have worked to develop a caring, loving friendship and life partnership where intercourse is but one of the indices of affection for each other.

Female Sexuality and Aging

Young women in western culture often experience far different sexual experiences than do young men. Many women who have reached maturity previous to the seventies may not have included masturbation and self-pleasuring behaviors in their developing repertoire of sexual behaviors. It is often difficult for them to express to their partners the desire for sexual behaviors that may not include intercourse. Early communication of sexual wants and desires permit the aging couple to share and enjoy sexual behaviors into their maturity without many of the concerns already expressed. When women marry previous to the peak of their sexual desires they may evolve a tendency to think of intercourse as something to "tolerate" in an effort to insure the faithfulness of their husbands. If early communication is not achieved these women may perceive the loss of their partner's ability for erection and penetration with some satisfaction and may, in fact, bring these behaviors about.

Female sexual functioning during the menopausal years is extremely variable and depends on the woman's general emotional well-being and her perception of life roles. Of equal importance, the abrupt cessation of ovarian functioning produces a drastic drop in the circulating estrogen and progesterone (Masters and Johnson, 1966). These endocrine changes produce in many women the physiological responses of irritability and depression. If the menopause occurs when other aspects of one's occupational index are in flux such as returning to school or career after children are grown, then complications may increase. If the male partner is experiencing a decline in sexual interest at the same time this may be perceived by the female partner as due to menopause, a marker of aging and perceived loss of physical attractiveness. After the fifties, the post menopausal single female may be depending on a dwindling supply of men whose sexual needs have declined markedly. If she elects to compete with younger women for the attentions of younger men she will very likely be faced at some point with the concerns of physical aging and the superficial contrasts with more youthful women.

A woman who has maintained regular sexual opportunity tends to maintain her sexual responsiveness; without such opportunity, sexuality appears to decline. Both men and women seem to attribute the cessation of intercourse to the attitudes or physical condition of the male partner (George and Weiler, 1981). Physiologically, females do experience some changes in vaginal lubrication and contractions of the pelvic platform during orgasm may be less vigorous and frequent (Masters and Johnson, 1966). Melman (1983) reports that diminished lubrication thought to be concurrent with aging may in many cases be attributed to treatable atrophic vaginitis.

Disability and Illness Affecting Sexual Functioning

Disability and illness is of course not limited to the aged. However, there are chronic and acute illnesses more likely to occur after age fifty. According to Crenshaw, Martin, Warner and Crenshaw (1978) organic impotence in the male may be secondary to such illnesses as *cardiorespiratory* (angina pectoris, emphysema, congenital and acquired heart disease), *endocrine* (obesity, diabetes, thyrotoxicosis), *genito-urinary* (prostatitis, carcinoma), *hematologic* (anemia, Hodgkins' disease), *infectious* (gonorrhea, mumps), *neurologic* (sympathectomy, parkinsonism, cord tumors), and *vascular* (arteritis, arteriosclerosis, embolus). In addition, drug ingestion (tranquilizers, and alpha-adrenergic blocking agents) may cause impotence.

In the female, indiscriminate hormone therapy extending beyond the immediate period of menopause has been thought by many physicians to promote a healthy-aging vagina. In fact, according to Comfort (1978), sexual dysfunction in the female due to failure of lubrication, atrophy and other local genital changes is probably a response less to estrogen deficit than to disuse. There appears to be a strong clinical impression that local application of estrogen with monitoring of blood levels is preferable to systemic hormone treatment.

Chronic illness affecting mobility in either sex such as arthritis, may require altered sexual positioning and activity for joint protection and avoidance of pain; but does not contraindicate sexual activity (Ehrlich, 1978; Halstead, 1978).

It is always wise to seek the advice of a physician concerning the effects of illness and/or medication on sexual functioning.

CONCLUSION

Two guiding concepts were employed as the foundation for a community based program in sexuality and aging. Wellness, representing a proactive balance of occupational roles and behaviors; and the need for the recognition of sexuality as a component of occupational behavior throughout the life span.

The PLISSIT model was used to structure a series of information and attitude adjustment programs focusing on sexuality and aging. Information was presented within a framework of occupational roles and behaviors recognizing individual differences and needs.

A broad perspective of sexuality was emphasized with recognition of culturally and socially defined maleness and femaleness through the lifespan. Aging on a continuum was also emphasized with no specific chronological markers for change.

A series of programs were provided for several community agencies: a retirement village, a senior center, a city parks and recreation short course, and three churches. All of the groups were responsive and interested and attendance remained stable for three sessions. The parks and recreation short course required a fee and continued for six shorter sessions.

REFERENCES

Annon, J. S. *The Behavioral Treatment of Sexual Problems: Vol. 1.* Honolulu, Kapiolani Health Services (1974).

Chipouras, S., Cornelius, D., Daniels, S. M., and Makas E. *Who Cares: A Handbook on Sex Education and Counseling Services for Disabled People.* Austin, TX: PRO:ED (1979).

Claman, A. D. "Introduction to Panel Discussion on Sexual Difficulties after 50." *Canadian Medical Association Journal, 94,* 207 (1966).

Comfort, A. "Drug Therapy and Sexual Function in the Older Patient." In A.

Comfort (Ed.), *Sexual Consequences of Disability*. Philadelphia: Stickley, 25-36 (1978).

Crenshaw, R. T., Martin, D. E., Warner, H., and Crenshaw, T. "Organic Impotence." In A. Comfort (Ed.), *Sexual Consequences of Disability*, Philadelphia: Stickley, 25-36 (1978).

Dahl, M. R. "Functional Restoration-Human Sexuality." In A. L. Hopkins and H. D. Smith (Eds.), *Willard and Spackman's Occupational Therapy* (6th ed.). Philadelphia: Lippincott, 447-452 (1978).

Ehrlich, G. "Sexual Problems of the Arthritic." In A. Comfort (Ed.), *Sexual Consequences of Disability*. Philadelphia: Stickley, 61-84 (1978).

George, L. K., Weiler, S. "Sexuality in Middle and Late Life." *Archives of General Psychiatry*, No. 38, 919-923 (1981).

Halstead, L. "Sexual Adjustment for Arthritic Patients." In A. Comfort (Ed.), *Sexual Consequences of Disability*. Philadelphia: Stickley, 85-88 (1978).

Johnson, J. "Wellness and Occupational Therapy." *American Journal of Occupational Therapy, 40*, 11, 753-758 (1986).

Kaplan, H. S. *The New Sex Therapy*. New York: Brunner/Mazel (1974).

Kinsey, A. C. *Sexual Behavior in the Human Female*. Philadelphia: Saunders (1953).

Kinsey, A. C. *Sexual Behavior in the Human Male*. Philadelphia: Saunders (1948).

Masters, W. H., Johnson, V. E. *Human Sexual Inadequacy*. Boston: Little Brown, 406-341 (1970).

Masters, W. H., Johnson, V. E. *Human Sexual Response*. Boston: Little Brown, 221-268 (1966).

Melman, A. "Common Disorders that May Affect Sexual Function in Women." *Sexuality and Disability*, 6, 2, 69-71 (Summer 1983).

Neistadt, M. E. "Sexuality Counseling for Adults with Disabilities: A Module for an Occupational Therapy Curriculum." *American Journal of Occupational Therapy, 40*, 8, (1986).

Newman, H. F. "The Pathogenesis of the Refractory Period." *Sexuality and Disability*, 7, 1/2, 15-16 (1984-86).

Sviland, M. P. "Helping Elderly Couples Become Sexually Liberated." Psychological Issues. In J. LoPiccolo and L. LoPiccolo (Eds.), *Handbook of Sex Therapy*. New York: Plenum, 351-360 (1978).

Age-Integrated or Age-Segregated Living for Semi-Independent Elderly People

Gloria Gallardo, BS
Margaret M. Kirchman, PhD, OTR/L, FAOTA

SUMMARY. Discussed aging theories supporting age-integrated and age-segregated living. Described supportive services needed for those living at home. The role of the occupational therapist was explained in both environmental options.

INTRODUCTION

In 1776, approximately 2% of the total population of 2.5 million people living in the United States of America were age 65 or older. By 1960 this percentage had doubled to 4% of the population. By 1980 11.3% of the population were 65 or older, and by the year 2000, it is estimated that 31.8% of the population will be 65 or over (Kapp and Bigot, 1985).

According to Freudenheim (1987), in the United States today there are 2.2 million people over 85 years old. In the 1990s that number will have doubled to 4.4 million and by the year 2000 it will have reached 5.1 million. The same article tells us that 13% of the elderly who are not in nursing homes have limitations in daily living activities. Since one-fourth of those who are over 85 are in nursing homes, a simple calculation tells us that by the year 2000 we can expect there will be about half a million people over the age of 85

Gloria Gallardo was a credit, nondegree student in the Occupational Therapy program at the University of Illinois at Chicago at the time of this paper. Margaret M. Kirchman is Associate Professor of Occupational Therapy, University of Illinois at Chicago.

who have limitations in daily living activities who are not in nursing homes.

Butler (1975) calculates that in 1972 6 million elderly people were living in 2.8 million substandard apartments or homes. In 1976 a Senate committee estimated that at least 30% of the nation's 23 million elderly — that is, 7 million people — lived in substandard, deteriorating or dilapidated housing (Growing old in America, 1978).

Thus there is a real need for housing for the elderly which is designed to meet their specific needs.

This article will address some of the questions raised in considering the problems of elderly people who are no longer able to lead fully independent lives, but for whom total nursing home care is not needed.

IN SUPPORT OF AGE-INTEGRATION

Theories of Aging

The question of whether housing for the elderly should be by age or integrated in a community where all ages are represented is basic to the decision about the type of housing to be provided.

If we adopt the activity theory of Havighurst et al. (1968) we regard optimal aging as characterized by maintenance of activity and resistance to the shrinking of one's social world. In order to age successfully, Salmon (1981) suggests that one must continue the activities of middle age as long as possible and find substitutes for the activities one is forced to relinquish.

Another theory of aging is the continuity theory of Atchley (1977). Atchley holds that as individuals grow older they are predisposed toward maintaining continuity in habits, association, preferences, and so on. Unlike the activity theory the continuity theory does not assume that the lost roles need be replaced.

Either the activity theory or the continuity theory can be seen as supporting the idea that elderly people may benefit from the presence of younger people in their daily lives and hence should not be placed in living situations where they are surrounded solely by others of their generation.

Kahana and Kahana (1970) found placement of patients in age-integrated wards led to significantly greater improvement in interactivity as well as cognitive functioning than placement in a completely segregated setting.

In an age-integrated situation the elderly person has the opportunity to continue the associations to which he or she has become accustomed and is to some extent, protected from the feeling of being discarded as useless.

IN SUPPORT OF AGE-SEGREGATION

On the contrary, Sherwood (1975) points out that fear of age-integration is often a by-product of fear of being victimized by young persons in high-crime areas.

The disengagement theory of Cumming and Henry (1961) which, according to Salmon (1981), views aging as primarily a process characterized by mutual withdrawal between society and the older person, points to restricting relationships, decreasing emotional involvements and reducing activity. This theory can be seen as supporting the advisability of age-segregation for the elderly, because in situations of age-segregation the elderly person is removed from the demands of society and the constant need to be involved in the activities and relationships of everyday living.

A second theory which may also support age-segregation is the social reconstruction model discussed by Bengston (1973). As older persons are exposed to negative attitudes toward aging (Salmon, 1981), they tend to internalize these negative feelings. This creates a need for helping professionals to assist the older person to reconstruct a positive self-image.

Either of these latter two theories of aging can indicate a need on the part of the elderly to live with others who are undergoing the same processes rather than to have to cope and perhaps compete with younger generations.

Twenty-five to 30% of older persons express a preference for age-segregated facilities (Sherwood, 1975). Rosow (1967), reports that residents of congregate housing facilities with higher concentrations of aged were found to show greater social interaction than those residing in housing having lower proportions of elderly residents.

THE INFLUENCE OF ENVIRONMENT

Recent studies have emphasized the importance of the environment as a factor in late-life adaptation (Hickey, 1980). When judging an environment, three criteria can be utilized (Brody, 1972): (1) the extent to which it minimizes the need for services, (2) how well it facilitates the development, maintenance, and delivery of those services that we require, and (3) how flexibly it can accommodate to the changing service needs of changing elderly individuals and populations.

Marlowe (1973) and Slover (1972) measured the environmental quality of many settings into which institutionalized patients were transferred. They found environmental variables to be more predictive of adjustment than the personality and development characteristics of their respondents (Hickey, 1980).

Numerous studies conclude that elderly individuals who reduce their negative self-concepts feel more in control of their lives and improve their functional independence with increased opportunities for self-control (Smith et al., 1986). It can be concluded that in planning housing for the elderly, attention should be given to providing for the need of individuals to continue to exercise control over their lives, and to feel supported in their perceptions of self-worth.

HOME CARE FOR THE ELDERLY

A national survey by Blue Cross-Blue Shield demonstrated home care is preferred two-to-one over nursing homes. A study by the University of Minnesota showed that 80% preferred home care (Freudenheim, 1987).

Care for the elderly in their homes is an age-integrated form of care because they remain in their home community surrounded by the usual cross-section of ages. Home care, by design, supports older persons in their efforts to maintain control over their lives.

For those elderly persons who wish to remain in their own

homes, some form of home care services must be provided, depending on the degree and kind of need of each person. Butler (1975) points out that the data strongly suggest that home care saves health dollars; for example, in one study in Rochester, New York, it was found that of the 1554 patients receiving home care in 1970, 653 (almost half) would otherwise have required hospitalization.

Growing old in America (1978) reports that Chicago was the nation's first city to establish an agency, the Mayor's Office for Senior Citizens and Handicapped (MOSC), to assist the elderly. It offers a wide range of support services. Some of these are available in the home; for example, nutritious hot meals are delivered. Recipients who can afford to do so are asked to share the cost; those who cannot, receive the meals free. Assistance in housekeeping, light repair work, shopping, and some meal preparation are supplied, and the recipients are asked to share the cost as their finances allow.

In Chicago, assistance is also available to those 55 or older in the purchase of wheelchairs, safety rails, walkers, and other prosthetic and assistive devices. The Department of Human Services provides funds for building ramps, widening doorways, lowering cabinets, and other remodeling designed to make the homes of the elderly safer and more adapted to their needs.

Health care in the home is provided by both nonprofit and profit firms, and while Growing old in America (1978) indicates that there are very real questions about the way these agencies manage their finances, there is no doubt that their services are of great help to their clients.

Day care centers also provide support for the elderly person who wishes to remain in his or her own home. Stroud et al. (1985) cite studies by Wan et al. (1980) and Weissert (1980) in which an experiment was conducted on the cost-effectiveness of day-care and homemaker services. Four groups were studied: one group received adult day-care, another received homemaker services, a third group received both, and a fourth, control group, received neither. On the whole, as might have been expected, those who received services did better than the control group, and those receiving day-care and homemaker services achieved higher levels on all measures of outcome than did those not receiving the services.

Hence, an elderly person can continue to remain in his or her own

home even when complete independence is no longer possible, if
the community in which the person lives provides adequate support.

GROUP CARE FOR OLDER PERSONS

Many elderly people cannot be supported in living in their own
homes; for example, they may have been living with relatives who
find they no longer can do the needed work. For whatever reason,
there are elderly people who must be accommodated in a situation
where other people are sharing the same care facility and care providers. This type of housing will probably be age-segregated; however, there are still many different forms it can take.

Public Housing for the elderly is not a service-delivery system.
No funds for service programs are included in the annual contribu-
tion from HUD (Lawton, 1980). This means that Public Housing is
not suitable for the elderly who cannot live independently, unless
there is a support system of home care for the elderly available in
the community.

Following are some examples of group housing for elderly people who need some assistance in the activities of daily living, but
who do not need total care.

A federally sponsored example of low-income housing designed
for the elderly and physically impaired is the Highland Heights
Apartments in Fall River, Massachusetts. This is an extension of
rehabilitation services of a chronic-disease hospital. The facility is
designed to serve physically impaired and elderly persons who are
capable of remaining in the community if barrier-free architecture
and adequate environmental support are available. Community and
institutional resources are coordinated to provide congregate dining
facilities, outpatient medical care, homemaking and visiting-nurse
programs (Sherwood, 1975).

Another facility is the Kissena Apartments in New York City.
The services provided include a senior center, a social worker available 8 hours a week, a moderately priced cafeteria, and limited
homemaker services. In addition, each floor has a chairman, one of
whose functions is to aid any resident in need of medical care. As
an aid in helping residents feel more in control of their lives and
circumstances, there is a tenant's council which represents the ten-

ants in dealing with each other and with the management (Herz, 1971).

A successful program of "intermediate housing" has been developed at the Philadelphia Geriatric Center. In all, 9 semi-detached one-family houses were purchased and remodeled to provide 3 apartments each with a bedroom, kitchen and bathroom. A living room is shared by all 3 apartments and for medical emergencies there is a telephone hot-line from each house to the Philadelphia Geriatric Center. The Center provides housekeeping and frozen daily main meals as optional extras at nominal cost. Tenants must retain their connection with their own physicians. The group programs of the Philadelphia Geriatric Center's Home for the Jewish Aged and of the Center's apartment building for the aged, York House, can be utilized by the intermediate-housing tenants (Brody, 1972).

IMPLICATIONS FOR OCCUPATIONAL THERAPY

The role of the occupational therapist in dealing with the elderly, as with any patient, is to prevent disability, to improve health, and to fulfill the patient's need by achieving optimal function and independence in the performance of the activities of daily life. In the care of the elderly the occupational therapist has the opportunity to use the widest variety of his or her skills.

The occupational therapist should be a part of the multidisciplinary team supporting an elderly person continuing to live in his or her own home. This involves, first, making an assessment of the condition of the client and of the approximate level of independent activity the person can manage. A program must be developed aimed at increasing and maintaining independence and providing mentally and physically stimulating activities.

The occupational therapist will also be concerned with making the home safe and convenient for older people who live with families, particularly in ways that will facilitate independence and minimize the strain on the younger members of the family who may share the home.

Smith et al. (1986) suggest the direction that occupational therapists should focus on in their treatment programs are the areas of occupation that improve life satisfaction by: (a) using activities that address the interests and values of their client, (b) using activities that enhance the self-image of the client, and (c) emphasizing work and recreation.

The occupational therapist who is working with an age-segregated group is basically concerned with 3 aspects of health care for the elderly: preventive, acute, and long term. Working together with other specialists, the therapist can provide different types of activities which aim to be physically, socially, and educationally stimulating, as well as assisting orientation (Redfern, 1986).

Kirchman (1986), in a study on measuring the quality of life of elderly persons, concludes that therapists should seek to minimize the effects of losses and compensate for deficits to enhance patients' effectiveness, support their competence, and help them maintain their self-esteem. In the group home setting this can be accomplished by treating the patients' needs on an individual basis and by group activity. These treatments will have as their goal meeting the patients' physical and psychological needs in order to improve both independence and life satisfaction.

Community resources such as theaters, shopping centers, or museums can be used to help extend the interests of the elderly client.

CONCLUSION

The elderly have much to contribute; they are rich in experience if not always in this world's goods. When the elderly are included in the life of the community they show improvement in health, self-esteem and activity level.

By continuing to be part of the total community the elderly may help to prevent misconceptions about the aging process and find living less stressful themselves. Age-segregated housing for the elderly may be advantageous by helping older persons avoid the misconceptions and rejections of younger members of the community. They also have less reason to compete with these persons. The advantage of age-integration over age-segregation is by no means clear-cut, nor is the answer necessarily the same for everyone. This is a question about which more research is needed.

The role of the occupational therapist in the lives of the elderly, whether they are age-integrated or age-segregated, goes considerably further than simply helping individuals to pass the time. Therapists can do much to help improve the quality of life, whether the elderly person is in their own home or a group home, by improving self-image, by raising self-esteem and self-confidence, and by helping to adjust to the aging process.

REFERENCES

Atchley, R. C. (1977). *The social forces in later life*. Belmont, CA: Wadsworth.
Baltus, M. M., & Zerbe, M. D. (1976). Independence training in nursing home residents. *Gerontologist, 16*(51), 428-432.
Bengston, V. (1973). *The social psychology of aging*. New York: Basic Books.
Brody, E. (1972). "Seeking appropriate options for living arrangements." In E. Pfeiffer (Ed.), *National conference on alternatives to institutional care for older Americans*. (pp. 147-157) Duke University.
Butler, Robert (1975). *Why survive? Being old in America*. New York: Harper Colophon Books.
Freudenheim, M. (1987). Insurance policies offered to help elderly infirm to remain at home. *New York Times*, no. 47,065, vol. CXXXVI, Sunday, March 1, 1987.
Growing old in America (1978), by the editors of the Chicago Tribune.
Harrison, C. (1968). The institutionally-deprived elderly. *Nursing Clinics of North America, 3*(4), 697-707.
Havighurst, R. J., Neugarten, B. L., & Tobin, S. S. (1968). "Disengagement and patterns of aging." In B. L. Neugarten (Ed.), *Middle age and aging*. Chicago: University of Chicago Press.
Herz, K. (1971). Community resources and services to help independent living. *Gerontologist, 11*(1), 59-66.
Hickey, T. (1980). *Health and aging*. Belmont, CA: Wadsworth.
Kahana, E., & Kahana, B. (1970). Therapeutic potential of age integration. *Archives of General Psychiatry, 23*, 20-29.
Kapp, M., & Bigot, A. (1985). *Geriatrics and the law*. New York: Springer Publishing Company.
King, L. J. (1978). Toward a science of adaptive responses. *The American Journal of Occupational Therapy, 32*, 429-437.
Kirchman, M. M. (1986). Measuring the quality of life. *Occupational Therapy Journal of Research, 6*(1), 21-32.
Kleban, M., & Liebowitz, B. (1975). Intermediate housing for the elderly: Satisfaction of those who moved and those who did not. *Gerontologist*, Aug. 1975, 350-356.
Lawton, M. P. (1980). *Environment and aging*. Belmont, CA: Wadsworth.
Layer, E. J., & Rodin, J. (1976). The effects of choice and enhanced personal

responsibility for the aged: A field experiment in an institutional setting. *Journal of Personal and Social Psychology*, *34*, 191-198.

Marlowe, R. A. (1973). *Effects of environment on elderly state-hospital relocatees*. Paper presented at Annual Meeting of Pacific Sociological Association, Scottsdale, AZ, May 1973.

Redfern, Sally (1986). *Nursing elderly patients*. Edinburgh, London, Melbourne, New York: Churchill Livingstone.

Rodin, J., & Larger, E. (1980). Aging labels: The decline of control and fall of self-esteem. *Journal of Social Issues*, *36*(2), 12-29.

Rosow, J. (1967). *Social integration of the aged*. Glencoe, IL: Free Press.

Salmon, H. (1981). Theories of aging, disability and loss. *Journal of Rehabilitation*, *47*, 44-50.

Sherwood, Sylvia (1975). *Long term care: A handbook for researchers, planners, and providers*. New York: Spectrum Publications.

Slover, D. (1972). *Relocation for therapeutic purposes of aged mental hospital patients*. Paper presented at the Annual Meeting of the Gerontological Society, San Juan, Puerto Rico.

Smith, N., Kielhofner, G., & Watts, J. (1986). The relationships between volition, activity pattern, and life satisfaction in the elderly. *The American Journal of Occupational Therapy*, *40*(4), 278-283.

Stroud, M., Katz, S., & Gooding, A. (1985). *Rehabilitation of the elderly*. East Lansing, MI: Michigan State University Press.

Wan, T. H., Weissert, W. G., & Livieratos, B. (1980). Geriatric day care and homemakers services: An experimental study. *Journal of Gerontology*, *34*, 256-274.

Weissert, W., Wan, T., Livieratos, B., & Katz, S. (1980). Effects and costs of day-care services for the chronically ill. *Medical Care*, *18*, 567-584.

Young, Pat (1984). *Nursing the aged*. Woodhead-Faulkner Ltd. Fitzwilliam House, 32 Trumpington St., Cambridge 6B21QY.

The Effect of Dying
and Death on Therapists

Kemper B. Martin, OTR
Cynthia M. Berchulc, MOT, OTR

SUMMARY. Physical and occupational therapists working in hospice programs are called upon to provide emotional support for their dying patients and their patients' families. However, therapists themselves frequently encounter a variety of personal stresses which often go unrecognized. Therapists treating dying patients may experience emotional, physical, and intellectual repercussions. This paper summarizes a review of the literature describing the effects of the dying patient on the caregiver. Descriptions of these effects and their impact on individuals are provided. The need for additional study in this area is discussed.

The growing numbers of hospice care programs has increased the numbers of therapists working closely with dying patients and their families. This paper summarizes literature that describes the emotional repercussions of treating such patients. Awareness of these problems may help therapists identify their own emotional and physical responses to repressed grief.

HOSPICE CARE

Hospice is a medieval term which refers to wayside inns for pilgrims and other travelers (Davidson, 1985). Today hospice has come to mean a palliative program designed to aid people in their

Kemper B. Martin is Staff Occupational Therapist, Department of Occupational Therapy, Memorial City Rehabilitation Hospital, Houston, TX 77080. Cynthia M. Berchulc is Assistant Professor, Department of Occupational Therapy, School of Allied Health Sciences, University of Texas Medical Branch, Galveston, TX 77550.

dying process (Barton, 1977). Dr. Cicely Saunders, founder of St. Christopher's Hospice in London, is credited for inspiring the hospice movement in North America (Davidson, 1985). Hospice philosophy today is "affirmation of life and a rejection of the presuppositions either that dying should be a taboo subject or that death is an unnatural event" (Davidson, 1985, p. 3).

Proponents of the hospice philosophy say that while dying is a normal process, many terminally ill patients and their families need support — physiologically, psychologically, and spiritually — to make the remainder of life as comfortable as possible (M. J. Towers, personal communication, July 5, 1986). According to Davidson (1985), hospice philosophy today has five basic principles:

- Dying is a normal part of living.
- Palliation is the treatment goal.
- Both patients and their closest companions, family and friends, constitute the unit of care.
- The spectrum of care should include support for survivors throughout their bereavement.
- An interdisciplinary team, including volunteers, is best able to provide the spectrum of necessary care (p. 3).

IMPACT ON THERAPISTS

Emotional Reactions

The occupational therapist is faced with three very serious problems when working with dying patients. First, the patient often experiences denial, avoidance, and anxiety. Helping the patient work through these issues is often very difficult and frustrating for the therapist who may question the value of these efforts. Second, persons in the patient's environment often begin to avoid or to become angry with the patient. These anticipatory grief reactions of others may result in the patient feeling rejected. The therapist may need to assist the patient in understanding his family and in interacting with them. Finally, the therapist is not immune from experiencing similar anxieties and feelings which may become so strong that the therapist avoids treating the terminally ill patient (Gammage et al., 1976).

An occupational therapist enters a hospice setting with his own beliefs, morals, values, and concepts regarding dying and death. Other attributes of the therapist, i.e., age, sex, educational level, religious convictions, experience with dying, and professional identity, also influence the therapist/patient relationship and may lead to conflict and stress. The therapist's personal attitudes and ability to face terminal illness and death also affect patient treatment (Kübler-Ross, 1969). "If this is a problem in our life, and death is viewed as a frightening, horrible, taboo topic, we will never be able to face it calmly and helpfully with a patient" (p. 31).

The therapist working with the terminally ill hospice patient faces a tremendous torrent of feelings stirred by this work (Barton, 1977). "Thoughts about death provoke anxiety in the form of fears: fear of the unknown, fear of impending loss, fear of change, and fear of isolation" (Gammage, et al., 1976, p. 294). Caregivers who work in hospice programs for long periods of time often begin to feel a sense of fleetingness (Barton, 1977). Some caregivers have described a sense of "I want to get the hell out of there." Others have complained of "nameless" feelings, i.e., feelings which lack words or symbolization. "Nameless" feelings may also include "'psychic numbing,' the process whereby there is interference with the ability of the mental apparatus to elaborate meaningful images and symbols related to life and the continuity of life" (Barton, 1977, p. 74).

Dying and death of patients is "a blatant confrontation on the part of the caregiver with his own mortality" (Barton, 1977, p. 72). The therapist may experience a profound sense of loss of control and helplessness as well as a sense of being professionally ineffective and incompetent. Feelings experienced by caregivers of the dying encompass virtually the entire range of human emotion:

> confusion, grief, helplessness, fear, anger, draining, loneliness, inadequacy, ambivalence, nameless feelings, intimacy, love, pity, needing appreciation, guilt, increased commitment, entrapment, needing release, superiority, lacking knowledge, intrusiveness, threatening, disintegration, wanting the person to live, wanting the person to die, protectiveness, abandonment, avoidance, alienation, lacking authenticity, intolerance, distance, and vulnerability. (Barton, 1977, p. 72)

Individuals experience these feelings at various times throughout life but the feelings are intensified when caring for a dying person. "At the deepest levels of investment in the dying person and the care situation, the person is aware of a sense of fleetingness, transience, futility, estrangement, and loneliness, and intense and often extreme sensitivity to loss" (Barton, 1977, p. 73).

While these feelings may be experienced in the therapist/patient relationship, they may generalize to other areas of the therapist's life. A therapist may react in three different ways: (1) the therapist may attempt to intensify other interpersonal relationships in order to attain a sense of aliveness; (2) the therapist may begin to perceive life as being mundane and of little value; (3) the therapist may romanticize death, intellectualize death, or turn away from the living (Barton, 1977).

Grief and the Caregiver

Kübler-Ross (1969) identified five stages of grief: denial and isolation, anger, bargaining, depression, and acceptance. Not only the patient but anyone involved with the dying person has to pass through at least some of these stages either prior to or following the death of the individual (Kübler-Ross, 1974). The process referred to as anticipatory grief, mourning before the actual death, may occur in many caregivers. "For the caregiver, it may begin with fleeting feelings of sadness and guilt" (Barton, 1977, p. 81). The caregiver becomes preoccupied with what he might have done differently. Any unpleasant interactions with the patient may result in guilt. "The sense of grief may be transient but it becomes particularly apparent in the presence of the person" (Barton, 1977, p. 81). "As the patient becomes increasingly ill, the caregiver must begin the process of letting go" (M. J. Towers, personal communication, July 5, 1986).

Barton (1977) found that caregivers are not given the opportunity to carry out their grief process. They often contain their grief and do not receive comfort normally obtained from others. The hospice caregiver may find it increasingly difficult to "let go" of one patient, only to face new relationships which will ultimately be lost again.

During the care process itself, the caregiver becomes aware of the losses that are taking place. These losses are recognized in the loss of

> the physical self, interpersonal self, the social self, and the potential loss of meaning derived from the relationship. . . . This reaction to loss and the sense of transience is at the very core of human existence, for in each true encounter and its loss there is a loss of part of the sense of self held by the person prior to the loss. (Barton, 1977, p. 82)

Grief in such circumstances is not only a human response, but an appropriate response and is a measure of the intensity of the dyadic relationship with another person.

Additional Stresses

A therapist's conduct while in the presence of the dying patient may also be a source of tension and stress for both the therapist and the patient.

> Our fear of saying or doing the wrong thing is exaggerated. As soon as the patient sees that you really care and that you, too, are human with human concerns, he will feel much more comfortable and will be much more able to share his own feelings. (Kübler-Ross, 1974, p. 109)

Many people working with the dying are afraid to laugh. However, acting naturally, laughing when things are funny and crying when things are sad, relieves tension both for the therapist and the patient, thus aiding communication (M. J. Towers, personal communication, July 5, 1986). Crying with a patient should not be considered as unprofessional behavior but "is rather a question of how much you are willing to share your own humanness" (Kübler-Ross, 1974, p. 107).

A therapist may also experience stress caused by changes in role expectations. For example, a therapist who is used to working within a medical model might encounter conflict and stress from working within the supportive and palliative model used in hospice (Davidson, 1985). The therapist may find it difficult to function efficiently as a team member which would negatively impact patient care.

Motivational Factors

The best way of overcoming one's own fear of suffering is to spend time with people who are suffering (Kübler-Ross, 1974). Many hospice staff become involved in hospice as a way of "resolving past losses, relieving feelings of guilt, assuming a sense of special calling, or proving that they can care for the dying better than others cared for their own dying relatives" (Davidson, 1985, p. 115). Mount and Voyer (cited in Davidson, 1985) suggested other motivational pitfalls: "having a hidden agenda, wanting to make this work one's whole life, and having unrealistic expectations or fantasies regarding the task, the team or their roles" (p. 115). Such individuals enter hospice care with strong needs not only to do the job well but to prove to themselves and others that they really are competent, which leads to extreme self-induced stress (Davidson, 1985). New members of a hospice team should be cautioned to avoid working with patients of their own age since the experience may be too personal and intense resulting in feelings of being overwhelmed.

Disengagement

A necessary but difficult step for the hospice caregiver is disengagement, the process of separating from the patient and "allowing a highly personal, internal, and subjective process to occur" (Barton, 1977, p. 83). This is a time in which the patient needs to be allowed to work through feelings about impending death. During this time, the therapist is likely to feel unneeded and abandoned and often begins to direct his attention to other areas to help himself deal with the pain (M. J. Towers, personal communication, July 5, 1986). The relationship enters "a realm which Kübler-Ross has called 'the silence that goes beyond words'" (cited in Barton, 1977, p. 84).

RESEARCH NEEDED

There is a growing body of knowledge describing the effects of the dying patient on the caregiver, but little is known about the effects of training programs designed to influence the attitudes of hospice caregivers. Tamlyn and Caty (1985) studied the value of education programs designed to help hospice volunteers confront their attitudes about dying and death. They hypothesized "after participating in this education program about death, hospice volunteers will show a change in attitude about death" (p. 37). The educational program explored therapeutic communication, loss and bereavement, pain control, and ethical issues related to terminal illness. The researchers reported there was a statistically significant difference between the average scores before and after the program, both immediately following it and six months later.

Future research is needed which investigates the effects of dying patients upon caregivers, an issue which impacts the lives of many health care providers. Possible areas of study include: (1) the effectiveness of education programs for professionals who work with the dying, and (2) the long term effects of grief containment on the health care professional.

SUMMARY

This paper has presented an overview of the literature describing the emotional responses which often occur within those who are working with dying patients. Individuals who care for the terminally ill need to be aware of their own physical stress responses in order to avoid unrecognized emotional burnout.

REFERENCES

Barton, D. (1977). The caregiver, In D. Barton (Ed.), *Dying and death* (pp. 72-86). Baltimore: Waverly.

Davidson, G. W. (1985). *The hospice* (2nd ed.). New York: Hemisphere.

Gammage, S. L., McMahon, P. S., & Shanahan, P. M. (1976). The occupational therapist and terminal illness: Learning to cope with death. *American Journal of Occupational Therapy, 30,* 294-299.

Kübler-Ross, E. (1969). *On death and dying.* New York: Macmillan.

Kübler-Ross, E. (1974). *Questions and answers on death and dying.* New York: Macmillan.

Tamlyn, D. L., & Caty, S. (1985). Hospice volunteers' attitudes toward death: Effects of education. *Dimensions in Health Services, 62*(6), 37-38.

FEB